Beginner's Guide to
WINNING TENNIS

by

Helen Hull Jacobs

1975 EDITION

Published by
WILSHIRE BOOK COMPANY
12015 Sherman Road
No. Hollywood, California 91605
Telephone: (213) 875-1711

To Hazel Wightman

```
Printed by
HAL LEIGHTON PRINTING CO.
        P. O. Box 1231
   Beverly Hills, California 90213
   Telephone: (213) 346-8500
```

SECOND PRINTING, DECEMBER 1962

© 1961, by Thomas Nelson & Sons

All rights reserved under International and Pan-American Conventions. Published in New York by Thomas Nelson & Sons and simultaneously in Toronto, Canada, by Thomas Nelson & Sons (Canada), Limited.

Library of Congress Catalog Card No.: 61-12638

MANUFACTURED IN THE UNITED STATES OF AMERICA

ISBN 0-87980-283-9

Foreword

Tennis is a simple game to learn if it is approached from the right direction. There are really no mysteries about theory, stroke production, co-ordination and strategy; nor about any of the other factors that combine to make a fine tennis player. I am going to try to prove that statement in this book.

It is possible that many of you have watched the present-day champions—both amateur and professional—and have seen them make the game seem easy to play; and then you may have tried to imitate their strokes. Perhaps, while you were doing this, you missed the ball completely, flubbed easy shots and found yourself in all sorts of physical contortions trying to get to the ball. The reason for this was that you started at the end instead of the beginning, and tried to match the champions' strokes without first laying the groundwork which is the foundation of the champions' games.

The fundamental purpose of tennis is to keep the ball in play longer than your opponent does. There are two ways of doing this:

1. You can play pat-ball, taking no chances, keeping the ball well above the net and inside the lines to reduce the possibility of errors. This makes for boring tennis for both players and spectators.

2. You can develop a forcing type of play which drives your opponent into awkward positions from which it is almost impossible for him to hit either a winning shot or to make an opening for the winner. Finally you force a weak return and have no trouble putting the ball away for a winner. With this kind of game, your speed of shot can often force an error from your opponent even when your shots are not well placed.

The forcing game requires touch, and usually an aggressive temperament and physical strength. But there are many players who do not have these qualities, and yet are equally successful with a strong defensive game. In many ways, a great defense is as powerful and winning as the big offensive game.

There is something else that lies behind these games which is sometimes more important than anything else. That is keenness—a real love of the game and of playing it, win or lose. This is the quality that inspires players at the thought of match play on great occasions, and lifts them to their greatest heights. This is the force, I know, that enabled me to win many a grueling championship match.

Too many players today feel that the game owes them more than they owe to it. They don't really know what it is to get a thrill out of tennis. They're missing a lot if they don't get as big a thrill out of their first small cup as they would if the national championship trophy, filled with flowers, belonged to them at the end of the tennis road.

Contents

Foreword		5
CHAPTER I.	The Basic Strokes	9
	1. Forehand Drive	
	2. Backhand Drive	
	3. Service	
	4. Volley	
	5. Smash and Lob	
CHAPTER II.	The Trimmings	49
CHAPTER III.	Position Play and the Spin of the Ball	54
CHAPTER IV.	Proper Timing and a Method of Acquiring It	66
CHAPTER V.	Doubles	68
CHAPTER VI.	Strategy	76
CHAPTER VII.	Ten Lessons for Juniors	80
CHAPTER VIII.	The Final Word	93
Glossary		94
Bibliography		95
Index		96

1. A.   Position when waiting for the ball.

Chapter I

The Basic Strokes

There are three major strokes: the forehand, the backhand and the service. In the average match, more shots are taken with the forehand than with any other stroke, so this may be said to bear the brunt of the attack. For that reason, a weakness on the forehand side is generally more serious than a weakness in the backhand. But since the backhand is generally attacked as a prelude to the advance into the forecourt, this stroke must be equal to the sudden test which is harder to meet at the moment than the test of control in a long exchange of forehand shots.

I had a long and serious battle with the forehand because I learned the stroke using a grip midway between the Eastern and the Western grips.

The first year that I was sent by the California Tennis Association to play in the National Junior championships, I had a strong Midwestern forehand. It served me well that year, although I was playing on a surface new to me — grass. On a grass court the ball hangs low, and I knew that the grip that I used was taking too much energy to stoop to the ball.

Although I won my first junior championship with the loss of only seven games, and the second with the loss of six, I knew that I had to learn to hit the ball with the Eastern grip. Bill Tilden showed me how. It was a simple change for it involved only a quarter turn to the left from my grip to the Eastern.

It took two seasons of play, however, before I felt that I could rely upon the forehand as I knew I could upon my backhand. Often, I used a slice forehand instead of the flat drive because against certain opponents who couldn't handle a slice it was the quickest way to win.

Because the average player's backhand is weaker than the forehand, most of the forcing shots are hit to that side by means of the forehand drive down the opponent's backhand line or the backhand drive crosscourt to the opponent's backhand corner. As a result, when a player can produce a backhand as strong as his forehand, he confuses his opponent by forcing him to alter his direction of attack, to make forcing shots in which he has less confidence; for example, the backhand down the line instead of crosscourt — a shot with very little margin for error. The fact that Donald Budge's backhand was stronger than his forehand was one of his greatest assets.

There should be no weakness on either side, for the backhand is no harder to make than the forehand. I think it is a little easier since it is naturally a freer stroke, because the arm is moving easily away from the body from the hit to the follow-through.

The service which puts the ball in play can no longer be considered the means to an end. It must be good enough frequently to be the end in itself. It must be an offensive, not a defensive, shot for players of the last thirty years have learned to take even the strong service as it rises from the court and pound out an ace. At least, they can make a return so forceful that the server is often put on the defensive when his service game should be a great advantage to him.

Strength and more strength must be the keynote of the backcourt game, and then the player is ready to go on — to add the finishing touches, the trimmings, to his game.

1. The Forehand Drive

In order to play first-class tennis you must understand all the strokes and how they are made, for each one has a purpose. There are three accepted grips for the forehand drive, the stroke used to hit the ball on the right side, presuming the

1. B.

the Eastern forehand grip—from above.

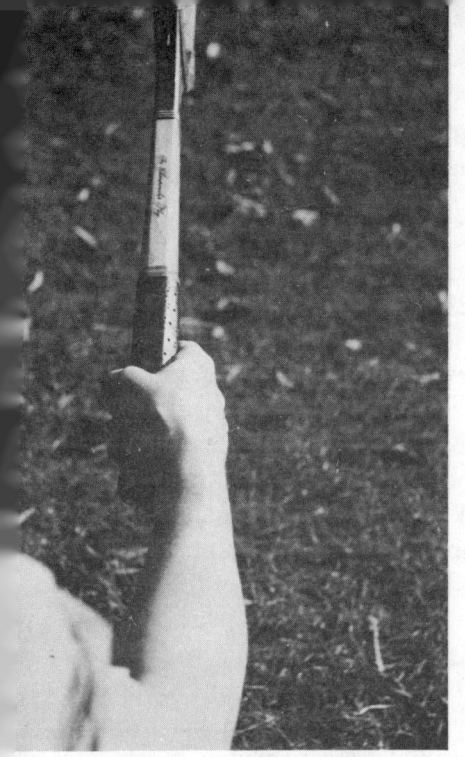

1. C.   the Eastern forehand grip—from front.

player is right-handed. These are the Eastern, the Continental and the Western. They are so named because of the places in which they originated.

The Eastern grip is the one which I favor and which is most successfully used by the average player. The four hardest-hitting champions I have ever seen play—Bill Tilden, Ellsworth Vines, Jack Kramer and Pancho Gonzales—all used, or use, this grip. The usual way of describing the grip is "...to shake hands with the racket." However, I found, when I was instructing beginners, that there was a clearer method. That was to put the palm of the hand on the racket face (the strings) and then draw the hand down to the end of the racket handle until the heel of the hand is firm against the leather strip at the end. Taking the grip in this way gives you more feeling of the racket face as being an extension of the palm of the hand when hitting the ball; and when you have this feeling, hitting flat will come more naturally. The wrist will be in its strongest hitting position, being flexible when necessary, yet firm when the racket strikes the ball. With this grip you will have as wide a reach as possible, and greater hitting power than with the other two grips. This grip originated in the eastern United States where the major tournaments are played on grass and the bound of the ball is generally low. But it can easily be adapted to a high bouncing ball, so it is the best stroke to develop for play on any kind of surface.

The Continental grip came into prominence when two great French champions and Davis Cup players, René Lacoste and Henri Cochet, used it with such success. After them came Fred Perry, England's world champion who was predominant in tennis for three years. With his rise, the popularity of the Continental grip increased tremendously. There is, however, one serious drawback to it which you will see if you take the grip. Stand the racket on edge and grip the handle so that the thumb extends across the front of the handle, the wrist is at a 45-

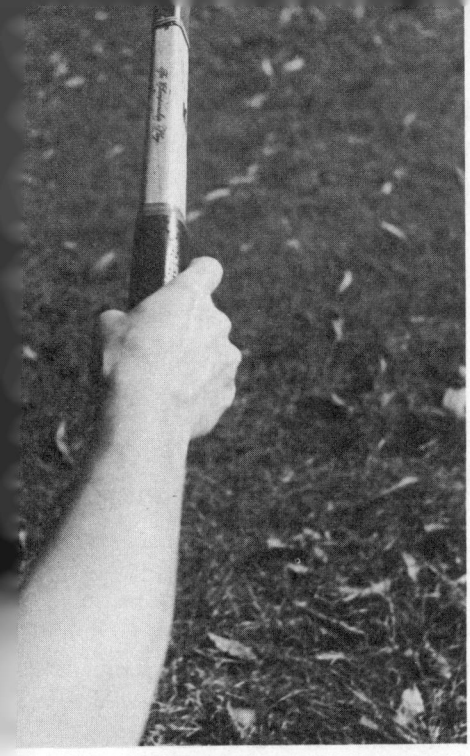

D. the Continental and the service grips—from above. These grips are identical. On the drive, there is no shift from forehand to backhand.

1. E. the Continental grip—from front.

degree angle to the handle and the palm of the hand is on top of the handle rather than behind it. Obviously, the effective use of this grip requires an unusually strong wrist, for the brunt of the impact between racket and ball is taken by the wrist.

Unless the wrist is strong enough to hold firm against the impact, it will allow the face of the racket to tilt backward as the ball is hit, and the result will be an undercut shot. The strings will draw across the lower surface of the ball, imparting a spin that is very risky — a sidespin, if the strings draw to the left, which tends to make the ball curve out, and a backspin, if they draw across the bottom of the ball, which tends to make it float.

On the other hand, the Continental grip allows a long reach and is particularly adapted to taking the ball early because the racket, when properly and firmly held, seldom varies from the vertical position, so that the stroke need not be so prepared as when using the Eastern grip. The racket face is always in hitting position. But I have noticed that players using the Continental grip who are forced to take the ball at the height of its bounce or after it has begun to drop do not hit with anything like the power of players using the Eastern grip; whereas, with the Eastern grip it is perfectly easy to take the ball on the rise as well, proving that this is the more successful all-round grip.

The Western grip was developed on the hard courts of California where the ball takes an unusually high bounce. Since the players who had to contend with these balls thought they could hit them more effectively when the racket was almost perpendicular to the court, they chose a grip with which they could comfortably move the racket in this position at shoulder height.

You can find the Western grip by holding the racket so that

1. F. the Western grip—from front. There is no shift from forehand to backhand. The wrist turns the racket over to execute the backhand. This grip is *not* recommended.

the strings are horizontal to the ground and then shaking hands with the handle. This brings the palm of the hand underneath the handle when the racket is in hitting position. With this grip it is easy to hit high balls down into the opponent's court, but as the bounce lowers, the grip becomes a disadvantage until, on grass courts, where the ball takes a long, low pitch, the grip makes for an awkward and uncomfortable stroke.

Since the severest hitting occurs when the racket face strikes the ball squarely from behind, it can be seen that the player using the Western grip would have to stoop tiringly to get the racket in this position on low shots. His only alternative would be to drop the racket head and come up across the surface of the ball, forcing it to spin rapidly forward. This forward- or top-spin, helps to control the ball, which tends to drop rapidly after it crosses the net. But at the same time, because any ball spinning excessively is strongly affected by air resistance, speed is sacrificed. Another disadvantage of this grip is that it considerably shortens the reach and leaves the wrist in a weak position on a shot wide to the forehand.

Now that you know what the three grips and their uses are, let us take the one which offers all the advantages and none of the disadvantages—*the Eastern*—and go on with the mechanics of the forehand drive.

There are three stages in the execution of the drive: *1. the backswing; 2. the forward swing; 3. the follow-through.* Every one of these stages is of equal importance in acquiring a powerful and rhythmic stroke.

Your aim is to hit a powerful shot from a given position in your court to a given position in your opponent's court. *But you must first learn to hit an accurate shot of moderate pace,* for only when you have got to the point where you can exchange a few shots in succession can you really appreciate the problems of footwork and body balance. Let us go through the motions of the forehand drive, to start with, as if we were on the court together. (See Figure 3.)

If you were going to throw a ball from your court to your opponent's, you would first draw your arm back, and as you did this, you would turn your body to the right. Why do you do this? To gather momentum for the throw. Then your arm swings forward, but when the ball leaves your hand, your arm doesn't stop. It goes on in the direction the ball has taken until your arm is fully extended. Now, a forehand drive is just as simple as this.

You are standing on the baseline, facing your opponent, who will be me, for the purpose of this explanation. When I hit the ball to you, *watch it very closely*, so closely that it appears to get larger as it comes toward you. *Just before the ball bounces in your court, commence your backswing.*

I will pretend that I have the power to stop the ball at this point so that we can study the backswing and the movements it entails. (I am assuming that I have hit the ball to you so that you do not have to run for it.) Without taking your eyes from the ball, *do two things simultaneously.* (1) *Step out with your right foot*, pointing it toward the sideline (2) *as you draw your racket back*. Do not draw it back too far, but just until arm, shoulders and racket are approximately on a line. The wrist is comfortably bent back, which carries the racket a little to the right of this imaginary line, and the elbow is slightly bent. Obviously, a totally extended arm in movement has not the power of the slightly flexed one. The racket head is just above the level of the wrist. The body has pivoted on the hips to the right as if the racket were a magnet drawing the body around with it.

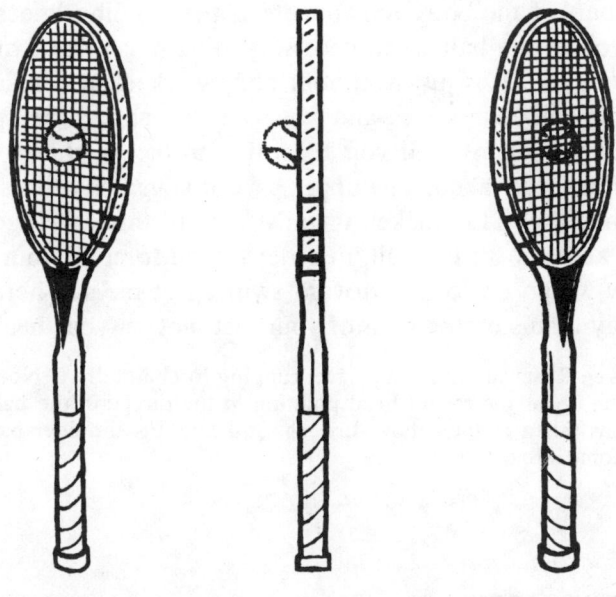

2. A.　　open face　　2. B.　　flat face　　2. C.　　closed face

Just before your racket begins to move forward, your left leg comes across to the right side, your left foot being about a pace ahead of and to the right of your right foot and at approximately a 45-degree angle to the net. Your knees will be bent, according to the height of the ball's bounce.

The reason for this shift of the feet and pivoting of the body toward the right is the same as the reason for turning toward the right when preparing to throw the ball. You are gathering momentum for your forward stroke and assuring yourself of good body balance as you make your stroke. All you have to do is try to hit the ball while facing the net with your feet parallel to know how difficult it is to make a powerful, accurate or rhythmic stroke from this position; and at this point we particularly want to get rhythm into your stroke, for it is the basis of power and accuracy.

There is another thing we want to do, and that is to assure that the center of balance is in the hips. In other words, the upper part of the body remains erect, the bending knees lowering you to the ball when necessary. *You never bend over to reach the ball.* It is just as if your body worked on coil springs that were in your knees and your ankles, and these springs elevated you or lowered you according to the height at which the ball is to be taken. The upper part of your body turns from right to left with the racket, its only forward thrust being made as you actually hit the ball, in order to add force to your shot.

Now we go on to the forward swing. Let me say here that you play tennis on the balls of your feet, not on your heels, for

3. Ken Rosewall makes a perfect running forehand drive. Note the tip of the racket head pointing in the direction the ball has taken at the follow-through, and how his shoulder has come into the drive.

WIDE WORLD PHOTO

you must have a quick and springy tread. You time your forward swing—and this means that you *must* keep your eyes on the ball—so that your racket face meets the ball at a slightly bent arm's length from the body and just ahead of the left hip. When your racket begins to move forward, your body begins its turn to the left, pivoting on the back, or right, foot. As this movement takes place, your weight which has, up to now, been on the right foot, is transferred to the left foot.

From the moment you place your left foot on the court in making the turn to the right until the moment after the ball has been struck, your foot remains stationary. It is only the right foot which pivots. Here, let me point out the analogy between tennis, golf and baseball legwork. *In all these sports, when the ball is hit, the player is really hitting against the left leg; and the left hip, to strengthen the position of the leg, is almost locked.* This firm placement of the left leg is essential to control because it prevents the body from turning too far to the left. Sometimes you see players in all these games take a terrific swat at the ball and then swing around wildly to the left. They look out of control and they are, because there is no stabilizing point in their body position. It is to curtail this wild swinging in tennis, as in golf and baseball, that a check is put on the body by means of the left leg and hip.

The line on which the racket is swung forward depends on the height at which the ball is to be taken. You have to learn, by watching the ball carefully, to judge the length and height of its bounce. You know, generally speaking, that if it crosses the net high, its bounce is going to be high, and you can anticipate whether it is going to hit between the net and service line or between the baseline and service line. But more accurate anticipation, which enables you to make unhurried strokes, comes only from experience and the development of your judgment.

When you have decided upon the point at which the ball

will be hit, bring your racket forward on a line connecting with this point. Unless you are hurried in making the stroke, there should be a *slight* pause at the backswing. This allows you to adjust your racket position in case you get a bad bounce or a sudden change in placement by your opponent. In addition, it gives you time to sight the ball with greater accuracy and to gather your force for the hit. It might be compared with a baseball pitcher's pause before he throws the ball. Under windy conditions this pause gives you a chance to bring your racket in line with a ball that is taking an erratic flight.

I mentioned that the wrist at the end of the backswing is comfortably bent back. As the racket is swung forward, the wrist straightens out so that it is firm when the racket meets the ball. Since we are discussing the flat drive, the racket face should be perpendicular to the ground at the moment of impact.

The next stage of the stroke is the follow-through—that movement of the racket and the body which lends control to your shot. Immediately after the racket has hit the ball, it begins its slightly upward movement. The body is still pivoting to the left. Racket and arm then continue until the tip of the racket is pointing in the direction the ball has taken. Often, the momentum of the racket head will carry it toward the left shoulder. This is acceptable, but what must be avoided is the racket action that takes the racket head *over* the left shoulder.

No ball crosses the net without some kind of spin. I am going to discuss spin in another chapter, but I would like to explain here that even the flat drive has a little forward- or top-spin. The ball remains on the strings of the racket a fraction of a second, which is enough for it to be affected by the slight upward movement of the racket which begins after contact with the ball. If you realize when you hit the ball that its surface has a top and a bottom, then you can easily visualize the racket strings moving up toward the top half. This movement makes the ball spin forward, but the spin is not pronounced as it is when the racket head hits below the center of the ball, coming up sharply across the part of the surface you can see. This latter movement creates the real top-spin ball which takes a high hop when it hits the ground, because of its exaggerated spin.

The tendency to be avoided in trying to hit the flattest possible drive is undercutting the ball. This is done by allowing the lower edge of the racket to incline forward, the strings passing from the center of the ball down toward the bottom. The result is that you force the ball to spin backward, or toward you, which reduces speed and control.

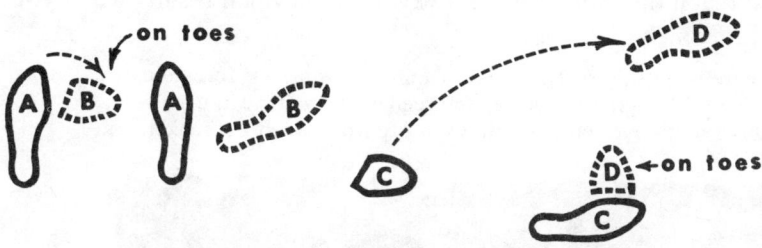

4. A-A.   Position of feet when waiting for shot on the forehand drive.
4. B-B.   First shift of feet toward the right.
4. C-C.   Position of feet as forward swing starts.
4. C-C.   Left foot swings around, right foot pivoting on toes as body moves forward at impact of racket and ball.

After you have learned to hit the ball that comes directly to you, you must learn to get into position for the ball to which you have been forced to run. There are different schools of thought in regard to the best method of approaching such a ball.

I mention Donald Budge quite often because his strokes are classic and could take any amount of pounding, in his height. Unless he had to scramble, he used the side-skipping method to get to the ball, so that he was facing the ball until he stepped into position to hit it.

Bill Tilden usually turned and ran with short steps which enabled him to change the position of his feet very quickly, if necessary; but he hit from a position more sideways to the net than Budge did. I usually turn and run to the ball, rather than using the side-skipping method, and when doing this, I step out first with my right foot. Unless the ball is very far from me and I have to run a considerable distance, I try to so time my steps that I begin on the right foot, step onto the left, then onto the right again, being ready then to begin my backswing. It is a valuable kind of rhythm of footwork: right, left, right and backswing, left and forward swing, hit and follow-through. Keeping this order in mind, go back to my description of footwork during the forehand drive and see what economy of movement this method offers. It avoids the tendency to take too many steps to reach the ball, and the awkwardness which results when you start on the left foot.

5. There is no sign of tenseness in Pancho Gonzales' forehand drive, although he has been forced wide to take the ball. Observe his eyes on the ball, even after it has left his racket.

Let me emphasize here the importance of keeping your body supple and your nerves relaxed. Nothing leads to cramped and ineffective hitting quicker than tenseness. You rarely see a champion tennis player suffer from arm or leg cramps, but today you often see players of tense temperament and unrelaxed bodies losing matches, sometimes by having to default, because of unbearable muscle cramp. Although this discomfort is attributed to diet in some cases, it is not always so. Just as often the difficulty occurs because the player has not learned the real meaning of relaxing, both mentally and physically, while under the strain of a big championship match.

It is impossible to overestimate the importance of watching the ball. It helps you to anticipate the shot your opponent is going to hit to you. And only by watching the ball can you make the type of shot and the placement that will win the point for you.

Lew Hoad demonstrates (1) the backswing, (2) impact and (3) follow-through on the forehand drive. This is a classic example of the stroke. The high follow-through indicates that he has put top-spin on his drive. The flat drive would have ended at least level with his shoulder.

2. The Backhand Drive

There are three grips for the backhand, which correspond with the three forehand grips, plus an additional grip which I recommend.

The Eastern grip is made with the thumb diagonally across the back, wide surface of the racket handle and the palm on top of the handle. The advantages of this grip are the same as those of the Eastern forehand grip.

7.   the Eastern backhand grip—from front.

The Continental grip is the same as the Continental forehand grip. It offers the advantage of long reach, but the disadvantage of a weak wrist position. As the hand is on top of the handle without the heel of the hand helping to support the racket at the moment of impact, the strength of the stroke depends upon an unusually strong wrist. The single advantage—the long reach—of this grip is not great enough to warrant its use, in my opinion.

The Western grip is the same as the Western forehand grip, the hand merely turning over to take the ball on the left side. With this grip, forehand and backhand are hit with the same side of the racket face. It is a grip which I cannot recommend because it is awkward, leads to the exaggerated use of top-spin and forces the player to stoop for shots below waist level. This stooping for the ball is exhausting in a long match and can make the difference between winning and losing.

The Midwestern grip is the one I most frequently use. With this grip, the thumb lies straight along the back, wide surface of the racket handle, bringing the arm almost at a right angle to the handle. It is only when a shot requires greater reach than this grip allows that the thumb shifts to the Eastern grip. I find that I get more power and accuracy with the Midwestern grip, which is so named because it is a compromise between Eastern and Western. The strength of the fist is added to the backhand with this grip, and the strong position of the thumb not only gives great support to the racket at the moment of impact, but also serves to help direct the ball when necessary.

Let us take the Eastern or Midwestern grip, and study the backhand stroke, which is executed the same way with both grips.

The backhand has one great advantage over the forehand drive. When the arm and racket move forward to the impact and the follow-through, they meet with no interference from the body. In the forehand drive the follow-through carries the racket and arm across the body. In the backhand drive it carries the arm and racket away from the body.

The best way to understand the difference between the reach on forehand and backhand is this: take your hitting position on the forehand and have someone hold a ball against your racket strings. Then, without moving toward the ball, pretend that the fence behind you is the net and move into your backhand hitting position. You will find that your racket face will reach to the shoulder instead of the hand of the person holding out the ball.

This difference in length of the reach of the racket and arm and therefore in retrieving can make a great difference in winning or losing a point, a game and even a set.

Perhaps the most important reason for developing a fine backhand is that many opponents neglect the stroke. So the average opponent's strategy and tactics don't consider the returns down the left sideline or short across court; or the lobs and volleys that can be made from a sound backhand. If you have an aggressive backhand, you can take advantage of this common weakness.

Like the forehand, the backhand should be versatile enough to be hit flat or with overspin. On some occasions, the undercut backhand is a valuable stroke. But use it sparingly, because an opponent going to the net against you can put this shot away for a winner if he takes it on the volley. The backspin of this undercut stroke means a slowing of the ball's speed, and that is what a net player likes.

Speed, disconcerting spin or placement can prevent the opponent from getting set for his shots. This means that he is apt to hit while off balance. And most shots made without balance are ineffective.

Some years ago the French champion, Suzanne Lenglen, the greatest of all women tennis players, and Helen Wills, one of the greatest of the American champions, won championships with few games lost because their backhands were indomitable. It was expected that their forehands would be great, and they were. But since their backhands matched their forehands, there was trouble for everybody who played them.

When the ball approaches on the backhand side, the natural tendency is to turn the body to the left so that the upper part of the playing arm and the shoulder are facing the net. This instinctive proper pivoting of the body is not always evident in taking a forehand, for beginners are inclined to continue facing the net even as the ball approaches.

In the case of the forehand these beginners do not get into difficulties until they begin the forward swing, whereas by facing the net on the backhand they run into immediate difficulties. They have to start by moving their racket across the body from right to left to reach the backswing.

The entire movement of the racket in relation to the body in the backhand, properly made, means free swinging and that is why I find the backhand an easier stroke to perfect and make with steady accuracy than the forehand. Certainly it is, at least, as easy a stroke to make as the forehand, so you need not share the average beginner's fear of the backhand drive.

The principles of footwork and body balance in relation to the movements of arm and racket are the same as those which apply to the forehand, only the movements are reversed. It is the left foot which takes the first step in running to the correct hitting position—about five feet behind and arm's length to the side of the point where the ball will bounce. It is also the left leg which advances, with the foot pointing to the sideline, as the body pivots to the left and the racket swings back in preparation to make the stroke.

Just before the beginning of the forward swing, start stepping into the shot by bringing the right leg across to a position a pace in front and to the left of the left foot, almost parallel with the net. As the racket moves forward, the body weight transfers from the left to the right foot, while the body pivots from left to right.

If the right foot is planted solidly on the court in the position described *before* the forward swing commences, the transfer of the weight exerts less force on the shot than it does when the forward swing is under way. It amounts to this: when your stance is solid before the forward swing commences, you are really letting your weight lean on first the left leg and then the right; but if you actually step into your shot, your weight is forcefully thrown into the shot.

In making the backhand drive, I always pivot well around to the left, so far so that occasionally my back is half-facing the net. This makes a longer backswing and consequently produces more power in the forward swing.

I keep my eyes constantly on the ball as I draw the racket back on a line with the point at which I anticipate hitting the ball. At the end of my backswing, the racket handle is at right angle to my forearm and my elbow is bent. As I come through in the forward swing, my body pivots to the right and my arm straightens out so that it is fully extended when the racket strikes the ball approximately a foot in front of and arm's length from my right hip.

The racket head is perpendicular to the ground at impact; then as I continue to pivot to the right after hitting the ball, the racket makes a slight upward curve to the follow-through, above and a little to the right of the right shoulder. On this shot, as on the forehand, I bend my knees to lower my body to the ball when necessary. In fact, even when taking the ball at shoulder height, my right knee is slightly bent. This flexibility of the legs enables me to get quickly back to position for the next shot, and also increases my balance during the execution of the drive.

My follow-through and position of the racket on the backhand as on the forehand, depend on the shot I have made. If I have given a slight top-spin to the ball, indicated by the upward curve of the racket, then the top of the racket frame inclines backward at the end of the follow-through. If I have hit the ball in a flat drive, then the racket face, at the end of the follow-through, is perpendicular to the ground.

It is just as important in making the backhand as in the forehand not to allow the upper part of the body to turn to the right faster than the arm and racket do. Otherwise, in the case of the backhand, the body turns against the arm and the tendency is to pull across the ball rather than hit into it.

Remember this: your body should pivot toward the ball, your body weight should move toward the ball and the power of your arm should be unimpeded at the moment of impact. In this way, you have put all your body weight into your shot and you are going to get the maximum pace on your drive with the minimum effort.

Until you have perfected the mechanics of the stroke, work

for accuracy, rhythm and timing instead of speed. There is a difference between speed and pace, for *speed* is the rapidity with which the ball travels through the air, and *pace* is the speed with which it comes off the ground after its bounce. Perfect coordination in the movement of your body and quick timing, *i.e.*, taking the ball as it comes up from the ground instead of waiting until it reaches the top of its bounce, give a shot pace. The force with which the racket strikes the ball gives it speed.

Never run around your backhand to take the ball on the forehand if it pulls you into your left court, for an accurate opponent will return by passing you down your right-hand sideline. In addition, this evasion of the backhand is likely to put you off balance and leave you vulnerable even to a moderately good return.

The only way you can strengthen your backhand and develop its accuracy is to use it. If you tend to run around it, your opponent will naturally know that you're afraid of it and he will build his strategy around that weakness.

Nothing is more important in tennis than sound and accurate groundstrokes. Bill Tilden once said that the greatest backcourt player could beat the greatest net player at their respective heights. I certainly agree. Bill proved it and so did Donald Budge.

For one thing, the powerful backcourt player can keep the net player from the net often enough to keep him from bringing his "big guns" into action. And if the net player goes in, regardless, he will probably find himself passed by skimming line shots or forced to scramble back by well-timed lobs.

Remember that every movement you make, and every forward motion of your racket must be toward your opponent's court. Keep on your toes and think forward.

No matter how much work you have to do on your backhand, it will reward you. And I can say from experience that when well made, it is one of the most satisfactory shots in the game.

Above everything, *watch the ball*. Watch it so closely that you can see it appear to grow larger as it approaches and smaller as it goes away. Players may occasionally hit the ball instinctively without looking at it, but this is not the way great shots are made and it is not the way to accuracy.

3. The Service

Because the service is the means of putting the ball in play and by its strength or its weakness you either begin a point with the upper hand or on the defensive, it is one of the most important strokes in the game. You want to develop a service that gives you the most power with the least effort. The best service is one you can make with consistent, moderate speed and pace throughout a match; yet one which can pound out an ace occasionally or at least make considerable trouble for the receiver.

I remember a match I played in 1928 against Mrs. Holcroft Watson, the English Wightman Cup player. She was a steady, hard hitter off the ground and I was getting very tired from my long backcourt exchanges with her. Finally it came to my serve at 5-4 in the final set. I felt that I couldn't survive another long rallying game with her, so I decided to put everything I had into my serve. I served three aces for 40-0 and had saved myself enough energy by then to win the following point after a long exchange. Had I tried to serve this fast throughout the match, however, I probably would not have been able to summon the strength at the end to serve those aces.

It is demoralizing to the opponent to know that he is facing a regularly powerful service. Realizing how difficult it is to break that service, he will expend any amount of energy to hold his own. He has the additional worry that you will choose to go to the net behind a fast delivery, forcing him to reply with a passing shot or an effective lob, and this puts him under a strain. But if you always hit your service as hard as possible, you not only take an unnecessary risk and expend too much energy; you permit your opponent the opportunity to get used to it. The value of Tilden's "cannon ball" service was that it generally followed a series of moderately paced serves. Or sometimes, he would hit a high-bouncing service and follow it by a cannon ball.

If you had watched Donald Budge serve throughout a match, you would have been surprised to realize, terrific as his service was, how seldom he hit for an ace. When he badly needed a point, yes; or yes again, when his opponent dared to move up on his second service.

You would have realized the same thing watching Alice Marble serve. She was often more effective when she served her moderately paced service than when she tried for an ace, for the percentage of "ins" on her hard first service was not sufficient to justify the toll it seemed to take of her energy during a long match. Of course, she could be devastating when she chose the psychological moment for her cannon ball.

Let us study the mechanics of the service. For this stroke, I use the Continental grip which gives greater flexibility to the wrist; and it is the action of the wrist, as well as the arm, that

8. Lew Hoad in the service sequence. The backswing (1) shows his weight beginning to go into the hit; (2) rising to the hit; (3) the follow-through showing considerable top-spin.

determines whether the serve will be hit flat, or with overspin, or with sidespin. I take up a position on the baseline with my left foot two or three inches behind the line and at approximately a 45-degree angle to the net. I place my right foot about a pace behind the left with my heels on a line. My right foot is almost parallel to the net, perhaps turned in just a trifle. My body is sideways to the net and my left shoulder is turned in the direction I am going to serve. As I prepare to serve, I hold the balls and the racket just in front of my waist on the left side.

The important thing is to throw the ball up to such a height that I will be able to hit it with a fully extended right arm at a point slightly in front of my left foot, so that I can throw my weight into the stroke. It is absolutely essential to master the art of throwing the ball up straight. For a long time I thought I threw the ball up straight until it was pointed out to me that I threw it well behind my left shoulder. Obviously, from this point, I could not move my body into the serve and my stroke lost power accordingly.

As you throw the ball up, two things happen: (1) your right arm drops in the beginning of the swing until it is fully extended behind your right leg; (2) your body weight shifts back to the right foot, your left knee turning to accommodate this shift. The racket does not pause in this downward movement, but continues from there in a semicircular upward motion to a position behind the head. At this point the body has turned sideways as well as bent backward to accommodate the motion of the arm. The forearm is horizontal with the ground.

A slight pause at this point in the stroke will allow you to gather your force and adjust your timing for any deflection of the ball because of toss or wind. Imagine that your elbow is on a spring, and that you are going to release this spring for the upward thrust of arm and racket after the pause.

You raise yourself on your left toe to reach the maximum height at the moment of impact, for what you actually want

Ken Rosewall is perfectly balanced for the service after the toss. Notice his left foot at a 45-degree angle to the baseline.

9. B. Vic Seixas comes into the hit with all of his body weight. Note that his right foot has come across to bring his hip into the shot, preserve his balance and start him toward the net.

WIDE WORLD PHOTO WIDE WORLD PHOTO

to do is to hit down on the ball, rather than to hit out at it. Just as you hit the ball, the racket head inclines forward, your body weight bends forward, and your right foot, having been raised from the ground by the forward and sideward bending of your body, swings forward to a position almost opposite your left foot. After impact, the follow-through begins, bringing the arm and racket down across the body. Your weight then falls upon the right foot which has come to rest slightly in front of your left foot.

Now let us go back over the various stages of this stroke. Above all, you want to gather as much momentum as possible for the moment of impact of ball and racket, which is the reason for dropping the arm to the fully extended position before beginning the upward swing.

The principle involved in the transfer of weight from the left to the right foot as the stroke is begun is exactly the same as in the forehand and backhand drives. *You cannot throw your weight into a shot unless your body has been previously resting on the back foot.* In addition to this, the playing arm naturally draws the body around with it, and as the arm swings back of the head, it would be awkward indeed not to bend backward to relieve the strain of the position. At the moment when the arm begins to swing the racket forward, the body, again naturally, must also move forward — but it moves forward almost solely from the hips up, the trunk being approximately at a 60-degree angle to the ground as regards its sideward inclination.

The forward inclination of the racket head brings the ball into court, and can be regulated according to whether your serves are going in or out. If they are going out, you probably need to incline the top of the racket head farther forward; if they are going into the net, you probably ought to incline it less forward.

But there is another factor that affects the accuracy of the service and this is the toss of the ball. If you throw it too high, you are going to hit it either at the very top of the strings of the racket or on the wood. In any case, it is not going to be affected by the inclination of the head and will probably go out. If you throw it too low, you will probably hit too much on top of the ball and it will go into the net. *Practice the throw until you can toss the ball to a point where your fully extended arm enables you to meet the ball in the center of the racket face as your trunk is inclining forward.* This applies to the flat service which has the greatest possible speed and pace.

There are, as well, the top-spin, or American-twist, and the sliced services. The same footwork, body balance and shifting of weight which apply to the flat service apply to the other two services. The only difference is that the racket face meets the ball at a different angle, and to make this change, the ball is thrown up to a different position.

1. *The top-spin service* is made by throwing the ball up to the same height as for the flat service, but farther left, approximately above the left shoulder. As the racket swings up to meet the ball, the upper edge of the frame is tilted slightly forward. The strings strike the ball just below its center and move sharply across and up the back surface. This action of the racket causes the ball to spin rapidly forward on an imaginary diagonal axis, so that when the ball hits the court, it takes a high hop to the receiver's left.

It is chiefly the wrist which whips the racket face up and across the ball in this way, although the arm, too, plays its part. The follow-through ends with the racket face well above and to the right of the point of contact. This service is particularly useful in forcing the receiver back of the baseline and obliging him to make a defensive return.

Even if the receiver moves in to take the high-bouncing service on the rise, he cannot make a very aggressive return because of the exaggerated overspin affecting the ball's bounce. This serve, placed to the receiver's backhand, is a good shot behind which to come to the net, for, even taken on the rise, it forces the receiver out of court when served into the left court, and into an extremely awkward position in midcourt when served into the right court. It is a very effective and reliable second service to develop, offering a striking and disconcerting change from the flat first service.

2. *The sliced service* is made by throwing the ball slightly lower and more to the right than for the flat serve so that the racket face can move down and across the outside surface of the ball. This service, after striking the ground, bounds low and sharply out to the receiver's right, and the ball tends to slide off the receiver's racket unless he is patient enough to wait until the spin of the ball is less pronounced before hitting. A slice, for this reason, is one shot that cannot be hit on the rise, being consequently a useful shot behind which to approach the net.

It involves so much risk if the receiver attempts a return down the line that the crosscourt return can be safely anticipated.

It is more valuable when served into the right than the left court. From the left court, the receiver, drawn by the bounce of the ball to midcourt, can more easily return the ball to either side. The sliced service is an advisable variation of the deliveries. Any change of pace and depth and spin which keeps your opponent guessing will help you to start your service games with the upper hand.

Remember that it is just as important to watch the ball on the service as on the groundstrokes, and that rhythm plays just as great a part in successful serving as in driving. *Throw the ball up high enough so that when you hit it at the top of its bounce (not when it is going up or coming down) your arm is fully extended.* By doing this you will avoid a cramped serving action and you will hit the ball where you can put most power into it.

4. The Volley

Now that we have studied those strokes which are the foundation upon which good tennis is built—the sound, powerful backcourt game—we can approach the net. You are prepared, in the first place, to force your way to the net when you have to, and this contingency often arises in a match. You may be battling your opponent on even ground in the backcourt, knowing that winning is a question of who makes the most winning shots, not who makes the least errors. In such a case, there is only one way to change the situation—the net attack.

I can give no better example of this than by referring to the Budge-von Cramm Davis Cup match at Wimbledon in 1937. Here was a case of both players being superlative from the backcourt. Neither one could hope for an error from the other, and indeed, the spectator could have counted the errors on the fingers of one hand. Donald Budge, who was the greater volleyer,

ASSOCIATED PRESS NEWSPHOTO

10. A.

Sven Davidson puts Ken Rosewall in trouble with a sharply angled volley. Davidson's balance and racket work are a fine example of this aggressive shot. Note the use of his left arm as a counterbalance.

realized that it was from the net that this match would eventually be won. In that stirring fifth set, of which Allison Danzig wrote so glowingly, Budge set upon the net, using the tremendous power of his backcourt game to pave the way. That decision saved the day for him and won the Davis Cup for the American team.

Important as the groundstrokes are, there is no place in tennis today for the non-volleyer. In the beginning of this book, I wrote of the value of the offensive-defensive game in which

10. B.

[Althe]a Gibson might have [gone] for the same attempt[ed p]assing shot that Sven [Davi]dson did. The similar[ity i]n their stroking, foot[wor]k and body balance [show]es the importance of [deg]ree in the execution of [the]shot.

WIDE WORLD PHOTO

the main purpose of the player was not to work toward the winning shot at the net. I will explain here that I do not mean this type of player is incapable of volleying. Even the good defensive player will often see and seize the opportunity to go to the net for the kill. Once at the net, the volley must be a punishing shot. The player who refuses the opportunity to go to the net, and when forced there, rapidly retreats, cannot hope to win today.

Personally, I prefer the aggressive type of game and had little pleasure in winning matches from the backcourt. When I was playing my best, I invariably planned an attack which brought me to the net. I am convinced that even for a woman this type of game is less tiring than running around in the backcourt. Although I was considered chiefly a backcourt player by some critics, my most important victories were won from the net.

I know it was largely my consistent net attack that forced my victory from Helen Wills Moody in the 1933 final of the American championship, although the match was won by default. Helen retired because she felt physically unable to continue when I led 3-0 in the final set. Incidentally, there were no holes in my forehand that day.

In the semifinal match at Wimbledon which I won from Alice Marble in 1938, I went to the net at every opportunity—principally to keep her from going up—and I think that any other course would have been unsuccessful. The net attack is invaluable particularly against players who do not like to make their groundstrokes in a hurry.

In playing the volley, the Eastern forehand grip allows greater reach and more flexibility of wrist than the Western. It avoids the evident tendency of the Continental to undercut the ball. The principles of footwork and body balance and weight-shifting which are the essence of good groundstrokes apply as well to the volley, although, of course, there are times when the rapid flight of the ball does not allow you to do more than throw your weight into the volley from a comparative standstill. You stand facing the net for the volley about midway between the net and service line. Naturally, on going in behind a forcing drive you approach much closer than this. But we are dealing now with practice cases in order to learn the stroke.

As the ball is hit to you, you begin your backswing which is the same as that for the forehand or backhand drive, except that it is shorter to compensate the diminished distance between your opponent and you. When you hit a volley at close range or are forced to take a low ball, you scarcely have time for, or want to make, any more than the slightest backswing. The action, in this case is more a blocking than a stroking, for you thrust at the ball with forearm and locked wrist. But when the ball comes to you above the level of the net, you want to hit with more power and accordingly your backswing lengthens.

As you bring your racket forward from the backswing, the shift of weight from the right to the left foot on the forehand volley, and from the left to the right foot on the backhand volley, takes place. At the backswing, which has carried the racket to a position in line with the rear shoulder (which, incidentally, has not turned as far around as for the groundstrokes) the wrist is bent back.

On the forward swing, the wrist straightens out to lock at the moment of impact, but it does not remain locked as in the drive. A continuation of its forward movement adds punch to your volley. The follow-through is short, ending in front of the left shoulder on the forehand, and on the backhand, ending when the arm is fully extended.

Of course, when the volley is blocked, the racket continues in line with the direction of the ball for just a short distance, perhaps two feet in front of you.

In all volleys, the turning of the shoulders toward the net and their forward thrust assist the arm and wrist in giving force to the shot. Generally speaking, the flat volley, that made with the racket head perpendicular to the ground, is the most punishing. Occasionally, on a ball taken well above the level of the net, slight overspin, created by tilting the top edge of the racket a bit forward, is useful. But even at this height, I think the flat volley gets better results.

Sometimes a volley, taken well below the level of the net can be more safely made with slight underspin, created by tilting the lower edge of the racket forward. Hit in this way, the ball is apt to take a low and sliding bounce in comparison with the higher bounce of the ball hit flat from below the net.

The drop-volley, which puts the ball just over the net, is made by tilting the head of the racket back just as the ball is hit. The follow-through is very short. This action puts considerable backspin on the ball, keeping its pitch very short after the bounce. The drop-volley is a useful shot when the opponent is in the backcourt, but very risky when he is in midcourt, for unless it is executed with perfect touch, it is apt to go too deep and, having no severity, result in a setup for the wary opponent.

For the shoulder-high ball I like the drive-volley, which is made with the longer backswing of the groundstrokes. Instead of hitting through on a line with the ball, I hit from above its center down into court. This volley should be hit deep.

The placement of all volleys is of primary importance. Because it is a severe shot made from close quarters does not necessarily mean that it is a winner in itself. Sometimes you will have to make two or three volleys before you get the chance to put one away, but it is a good plan to make your first one deep into either corner to open the court for your shorter angled volley. If you are coming into the net and your first volley is angled when you are still on the move, your opponent has the chance of passing you with an equally sharp, angled drive. Whereas, if your first volley is deep to the corner, you are entrenched at the net and in better position to cover his angled return by the time he has hit it.

Some players favor the center theory—that is, making the volley to the center of the backcourt, thereby reducing the possible angle of the opponent's return. Some players use this center volley against an opponent who does not like to hit the ball when it is close to him. The volley to the corner, however, means that the opponent's shortest return is down the line, a risky shot which you automatically cover by coming in more to that side than the center of the net. If he does return crosscourt, taking longer to reach the net, you have time to cross over and volley down his unguarded sideline. When he is trying to pass you from the center of the court, his angles of return may be limited, but you have also cut down your possibilities of volleying the ball out of his reach.

Basically speaking, the volley should be the finishing shot. The minute your opponent gives you a ball in midcourt, you have your signal to drive deep and hard and go to the net. If you plan your backcourt game around the desire to get to the net to finish the point, you will play more aggressively from the baseline. Instinctively, you will move forward as you hit, ever alert for the weak return, and this, in itself, will add power to your hitting.

It is important to remember that once you get to the net you must not volley tentatively. If your opponent knows that you volley to end the point, he will press on his passing shot—and pressing breeds errors.

There is no need to point out how important it is to watch the ball on the volley. The ball is hit in front of you. You aim it, and that means watching it onto the racket strings at the point you have chosen to hit it. *Here, as in making the drives, your bending knees lower you to the ball.* A volley made off balance, which so easily happens if you bend over from the waist to reach the ball, leaves you helpless in the face of the opponent's return. The left arm, used as a counterbalance, helps to balance the body for a volley just as it does for the other strokes of the game. If you are forced to leap to the ball to reach it, out goes the left arm automatically.

In the volley, as in the other strokes, cultivate grace through rhythm. It is the invariable quality which all great champions have in common.

ASSOCIATED PRESS NEWSPHOTO

11. Only with perfect balance could Ken Rosewall make this low volley. Both left leg and left arm are the counterbalances in this shot.

5. The Smash and the Lob

The smash is, in effect, a serve for which your opponent has tossed up—or lobbed—the ball. It is made in the same way as the serve with this exception: you may often be on the move when making it. Let us first study the smash which you can make without altering your position. You are at the net. Your opponent lobs—that is, hits the ball over your head. Your first movement is a pivot to the right as your arm drops. Then the racket begins its upswing, the upper part of your body bending back to accommodate this drawing back and raising of the racket.

WIDE WORLD PHOTO

12.   Sometimes on the overhead smash the outward movement of the racket face is necessary to hit the ball away from the opponent. Ham Richardson does it here against Rosewall.

The next movement is the raising of the body on the toes of the right foot which will enable you to hit the ball at the top of your swing and at the same time be certain that the full weight of your body goes into the shot. As your arm straightens for the impact, the weight transfers from the right to the left foot, and then you bring the racket down across the body in the follow-through.

Now, your opponent may toss up a lob that forces you back. The only way to develop your judgment of the depth and height of the ball and how far you have to go to cover it is to practice against lobs. But when you have developed this judgment, even in a small degree, you will know that it is wiser to turn around and run back, watching the ball over your shoulder, than to run backward on your heels. Then, as you turn around to take the ball, you go through the same motions as I have previously described. Sometimes, instead of merely raising the body on the right toe, you may have to leap into the air off the right foot to reach the ball at the top of your swing if (a) you have misjudged its depth or (b) you have been caught so close into the net that you are unable to cover the ball except by leaping up for it.

13. The smash, taken in mid-air by Alex Olmedo, is an example of arm and shoulder coming into the shot while the legs help to maintain balance.

WIDE WORLD PHOTO

A very deep lob is better taken after allowing the ball to bounce; but remember that wherever you take it, the principles of shifting and throwing the weight into the shot by means of the pivot and the forward inclination of the trunk, and rhythm make the shot a winner. You may have the arm of a longshoreman, but it cannot do all the work, and why should you want it to when you can add to it the power of your co-ordinated body weight?

Whether you take the ball with or without leaping for it, practice timing the stroke so that you are not hitting the ball behind your head, or, on the other hand, too far out in front of you. *And when you hit the ball, do not make your shot tentative.* Try to kill it, to win outright with it, for that will discourage your opponent from subjecting you to a lobbing attack; whereas, if you hit your overheads timidly, giving your opponent the opportunity to return the ball, you will find that he will use the lob as a means of tiring you. It is better to miss a few, getting your range and your touch, than to push them back into your opponent's reach.

14. Lew Hoad's backhand smash is made with arm and shoulder power, which can be done only with the right foot leading.

WIDE WORLD PHOTO

On the other hand, when you go to the net, do not try to avoid the lob by hanging back. All you do in such a case is to decrease the power and effectiveness of your volley. Go up within, say, three feet of the net, but be ready to drop back for the lob, which you will learn to anticipate from the position of your opponent's racket and the action of his arm preparatory to making the lob. Since he has to hit from beneath the ball with an open-face racket, and, generally speaking, make the shot slowly in order to place it accurately; you will know when it is coming.

WIDE WORLD PHO

15. A. Caught on the baseline, Pancho Gonzales lobs—the right defense when in trouble.

The lob can be an aggressive shot, particularly when its trajectory is long and just high enough to pass out of reach of the opponent. This lob, after bouncing, pitches toward the baseline or the fence, making a return almost impossible.

Bobby Riggs, one of the most astute of the American cham-

WIDE WORLD PHOTO

15. B.

The backhand lob by Lew Hoad shows the perfect position of the racket just after the impact. Note his eyes following the ball. This lob was obviously a defensive one, for he is going backward as he hits it.

pions, turned the high lob into an aggressive shot by placing it in the corners of his opponent's court. This he had learned to do with such accuracy that he scarcely ever made an error. Occasionally, he lobbed to gain time or to regain his court position, but more often he used it in the midst of a driving rally as an unpleasant surprise against an adversary.

George Lott, an outstanding American doubles champion, and my partner when we won the national mixed doubles in 1934, had perhaps the best lob of all. Frequently he surprised me when I thought he was going to drive against our opponents by going for the ball as if to drive and suddenly lofting it over the heads of the players at the net. By the time they had decided who was to run for it, the ball had usually bounced into the backstop.

He was able to disguise it well, because since he used the Western top-spin forehand and backhand, he could hit the lob with a stroke that closely resembled his drive. He hit the ball with considerable overspin which caused it to pitch rapidly forward after bouncing. Sometimes he undercut the ball by hitting across the under surface of the ball from back to front.

A lob so hit hangs in the air longer than the top-spin lob and is really only useful in giving the player time to regain his court position.

The more you are able to disguise your lob, making the stroke resemble your drive by opening the face of your racket at the last minute to loft the ball into the air, the more chance you have of successfully confusing your opponent, of winning the point outright by a shot so sudden that he cannot possibly get back to it in time.

I will discuss the use of the lob more fully in the part of this book devoted to strategy.

Chapter II

The Trimmings

The strokes which are the trimmings of a sound tennis game and are learned only after you have mastered the foregoing fundamental ones are the *slice*, the *chop*, the *half-volley* and the *drop-shot*. It is possible to win without these shots, but complete knowledge of the game and the use of all the shots is tennis in its highest form. This was demonstrated beyond question by the greatest champion of all, Bill Tilden, who was able to win Wimbledon at thirty-seven, ten years after his first victory there, and was the first-ranking player in the United States for ten years. None of the champions since Tilden's day have coped with the number of great players at their height that he did. Bill Johnston, Vincent Richards, Henri Cochet, Jean Borotra, René Lacoste, to name a few, all tested the power and versatility of Tilden's game and found that he had all the answers to their methods of attack and defense. Where other players were satisfied to attack or to defend only, Tilden could break down a seemingly sound game with his variation of pace and spin and depth and then put on the pressure to finish it off. He was equally at home in the backcourt or the forecourt,

WIDE WORLD PHOTO

16.

oming in on the full run for e volley, Tony Trabert will level with Vic Seixas for e "tandem" doubles position. o holes are left in their court.

the only sign of a weakness in his game being, perhaps, the overhead smash. And this stroke was weak only by comparison with the greatest smashes of the day.

There is a tendency today to underestimate the value of the slice and the chop. The exclusive use of either is a great mistake, chiefly for the reason that they are almost useless as passing shots, and also because neither carries the speed or pace of the drive. But used wisely, as a change of pace and spin, or to upset the timing of the automatic driver, they are a very valuable adjunct to anyone's game.

Let us study the mechanics of the two strokes.

The slice is made with the Continental grip. The footwork, body-pivoting and transfer of weight which govern the drives apply also to this stroke. The backswing is higher and shorter than for the drive and the racket face, instead of being vertical, is open — the upper edge of the racket head tilted back. The head comes through in this position on the forward swing, striking the ball down across its back, under surface. This action imparts backspin, causing the ball to travel through the air longer than the flat or top-spin drive. The bounce of the ball is low and skidding. If hit by the opponent before the spin has decreased, the ball is apt to slide off his racket. For this reason, the slice forces the opponent to delay his stroke and is particularly upsetting to one who likes to take the ball on the rise.

The arm action in making the slice is very important. The overuse of the wrist, a great temptation, must be avoided. The forearm moves through on the forward swing faster than the upper arm and is the prime force in making the shot. The wrist, by its downward motion on the forward swing adds strength that increases the backspin. Players who slice ineffectively usually do so because they try to impart the spin by the sharp downward action of the wrist alone. *The shifting weight, the pivoting trunk and the well-timed arm action must contribute* to the pace of the slice to produce those low, deep, skidding shots that may be successfully followed to the net.

A short slice, unless hit sharply crosscourt when the opponent is hovering on the baseline, has little value.

The sliced drive when it is hit deep can be very troublesome, even to a good driver. I often used it to break up an opponent's driving attack, especially when that player liked to maintain rhythm in her driving. I used it, too, when I found that a driving approach to the net did not prevent my opponent's ball from passing me as I came in. The slice, at least, slowed down her return and gave me a chance to take up the net position before the ball could go by me. But by overuse I often broke the timing on my forehand drive; so when my opponent approached the net, I had no suitable passing shot myself. This is the reason I so strenuously emphasize that the slice should be reserved for its proper use.

17. A., B.   Pancho Gonzales executes an aggressive backhand slice.

The chop is made with the Eastern grip and the action is the same as that in chopping wood. The stroke is short, beginning with bent arm above the right shoulder and coming sharply down the back surface of the ball. The movement of body and feet should be identical to that for the drives, for here, again, the weight and forward movement of the body must add power to the shot. The follow-through is short, ending in front of the extended left leg on the forehand and the right leg on the backhand. The downward movement of the wrist from cocked position at the backswing to the follow-through is also considerably shorter than in hitting the slice.

The chopped ball has a short pitch after bouncing, and its flight through the air is slower than the slice. *In comparison with the slice, I believe it is a better shot for the angled, cross-court return, but is less effective as a deep shot.* Its spin is not so disturbing as the slice since it is inclined to "sit up" too much.

The chop is akin to the drop-shot, which is made the same way, so far as grip and stroke action are concerned. But in order to drop the ball just over the net it's hit more slowly and with delicacy rather than force. The drop-shot is easier to make if the ball is taken on the rise because, the forward spin being then more pronounced, your drop-shot stroke merely neutralizes the spin. And when you neutralize the spin of the ball without then adding any more, the ball tends to drop dead over the net. If you wait longer than this to hit the ball, you will impart more backspin to it, but you will also risk the ball's taking a higher and deeper flight.

The drop-shot is useless unless it lands close to the net and is played when the opponent is in the backcourt. Otherwise it leaves you open to a drop-shot in return or a kill by your opponent. *The drop-shot hit to either side rather than the middle of the court is most useful, if for no other reason than that the net is higher at the sides, adding a little to the possibility of error on the return.*

As with the slice and chop, its use should be judicious. The best drop-shot in the world can be anticipated to some extent, but anticipation doesn't help the opponent if he is beyond possible reach of it.

The only misnamed shot in the game is the half-volley, which has nothing at all to do with volleying. It is a shot taken on the backhand or forehand side, with the same grips used for the drive, immediately after the ball has bounced. Both backswing and follow-through are shortened for the shot until, when taking the ball close to the net, there is practically no preparation for the stroke at all. Your racket merely drops behind the ball, the ball then hitting the strings with hardly any motion of the racket. The principles of shifting weight and footwork when deliberately making a half-volley in back- or midcourt must be observed. The closer you approach the net when making this shot, the more careful you must be that the racket face is slightly tilted back to permit the ball to clear the net.

While the half-volley was used as a deliberate means of attack by such players as Fred Perry and Henri Cochet because it enabled them either to hurry their opponents or to get to the net more quickly themselves, *it should, generally speaking, be reserved for emergencies.* When you are coming in to the net and the ball is hit at your feet, or when a ball approaches you so quickly in the backcourt that you have not time to take it with the drive, the half-volley is the answer.

Chapter III

Position Play and the Spin of the Ball

Your aim on the court should be to reduce the possible angles of your opponent's returns—not in relation to the court, but in relation to your own position in court. In other words, if you are standing in your backhand corner and your opponent hits the ball to that corner, the angle is wide, in relation to the court, but not wide in relation to your position.

Say you are receiving in the right-hand court and your opponent serves to your forehand. Your seemingly obvious return is down the line to his backhand corner, but in making this return, you open up your own backhand corner to his return. I have seen a great many good players run afoul of Donald Budge's backhand by making such a return. In addition to this you run the risk of having to make a difficult return of your opponent's crosscourt shot; that is, the service to your forehand.

I have found that if I return the serve to my forehand short across court to my opponent's forehand and then, regardless of his return, make my next return to his backhand corner, I put him into more difficulty than I do with the return down the line. Why is this?

After serving to my forehand, the opponent is naturally on the watch for the backhand return. At the end of his follow-through, he moves more easily to the left than to the right; but the deep backhand after the short crosscourt forehand is a most difficult shot to cover. It all resolves itself into a question of angles.

If, instead of remaining in the backcourt after receiving service, you go to the net to volley, then your next return is best made down the sideline, because it reduces the possibility of a passing shot. Look at Figures 18 and 19. In Figure 18 the return has been made down the line from A to B, and you have taken up a volleying position at C, which is slightly to the right of the center service line. From this position you are able to cover the shortest return—that down the line, and you will have time to move over to cover the longest return, across court from B to E.

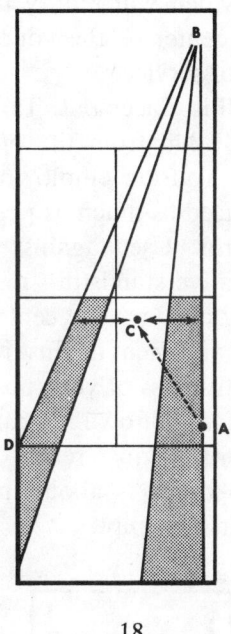

18.

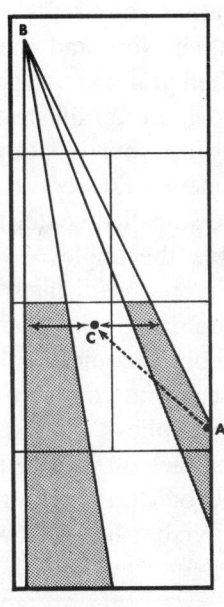

19.

Now study Figure 19. You have returned the ball from A to B. In order to be in position to cover your opponent's return down the line, you must run up approximately to the point marked C at the net. This point is, of necessity, a little to the left of the center service line.

To cover the shortest return your opponent can make—the one which will send the ball back to you the soonest—you have had to run farther than to cover the similar shot in Figure 18. In addition to this, you have forced yourself to volley the ball coming to you down the line with the backhand instead of the forehand, and you have given your opponent the opportunity to make this shot down the line with his forehand. In Figure 18 he has had to make the shot with the backhand.

These facts apply to the return of service from the left corner of the left service court. But you must remember not always to play the same return, or you will find your opponent anticipating your reply and preparing for it, which will nullify its value. Now and then hit deep down the center of the court, when you want to go to the net on return of service.

Figure 20 illustrates the advantages of this placement. Taking up your position at C, you are equidistant from the opponent's crosscourt returns to either side. You are employing the so-called center theory, which has reduced as much as possible the angles of your opponent's returns. Used against a player who dislikes to hit from a comparative standstill — one who does not well return a ball hit directly at him — the center theory becomes doubly effective. The chief argument against its use is that you have also reduced the effectiveness of your possible volleys, having diminished the angles for your own returns. You are playing to an opponent who is within equal reach of the ball on fore- or backhand. The drop-volley is about the only shot likely to win the point on the first attempt.

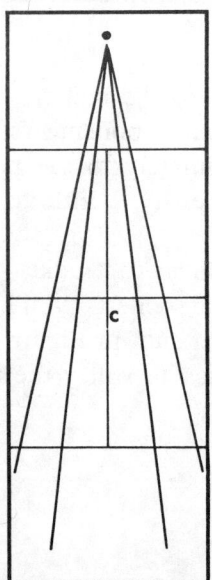

20.

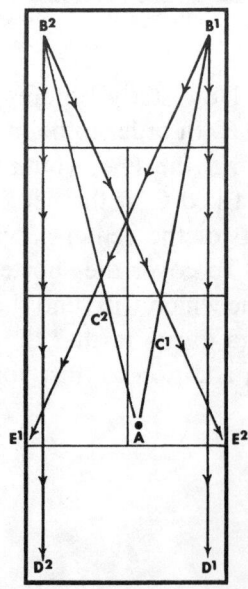

21.

In Figure 21 we are concerned with the return of service to the center service line. In this case whether you return the ball to the right or left corner of your opponent's court is really immaterial, for you have been drawn to the middle of the court to make the return and are therefore more or less equidistant from C^1 and C^2, your volleying positions.

If you are receiving in the right court, it is a bit more difficult to make a backhand return to B^2 than to B^1. If you are receiving in the left-hand court, it is a little easier to make your forehand return to B^1 than B^2, although the return to B^2 from either side will come easily enough with placement practice. When your opponent is serving from his right-hand corner, he is somewhat nearer B^2, but is usually on the watch for the return to his backhand.

You will notice in all these diagrams that your volleying position is at the bisection of the angle of widest possible returns. In other words, in Figure 21 if you hit the ball to B^1, the widest return your opponent can make crosscourt is B^1-E^1; the farthest return from you on the other side is B^1-D^1. These lines, meeting at B^1, form an angle which you bisect by taking up your position at C^1. By bisecting this angle you are equidistant from both returns. Although this may seem complicated to you, remember that it is the basis of good position play in any part of the court—whether you are volleying from the net or driving from the backcourt. Practice and experience teach you to choose these positions instinctively. You may not move accurately into them, but you will be near enough to reduce the effectiveness of your opponent's angled returns.

While you strive to reduce your opponent's possible angles, you want to increase your own, at the same time, opening up his weakness. Say he is weak on the backhand. You don't want to start in hammering away at his backhand corner, for by doing this you enable him either to run continually around the backhand, or to improve it by constantly hitting it.

In nine cases out of ten, you can win a point more quickly by playing through your opponent's strength to his weakness. Start out by drawing him over to his forehand side. If you hit two or even three shots to that side, he is apt to grow careless about protecting his backhand corner. Then comes your opportunity to drive into his backhand and go to the net. The same tactics apply in reverse where the opponent's forehand is his weakness. But in using these tactics you must be certain that your position play is good in order to protect yourself against his strength while you are exposing his weakness. That is why the theory of bisecting the angle is so important in the backcourt, too.

Your correct court position after each shot made from the backcourt is a few feet behind the center of the baseline. Don't be lazy about getting back into this position. If you are, a quick player will beat you on position play alone, taking the ball on the rise to shoot it past you before you can get within reach of it. From the center of the baseline, as your return drops into the opponent's court, you are able to move easily either way into the position that bisects the angle of his returns. The player who makes a difficult recovery of a shot that has drawn him out of court, and then waits to see whether his return is going in before getting back into position is easy prey to a player like Fraser or Gonzales.

When you are fortunate enough to be given a shot in midcourt, take instant advantage of it. There is only one reply to such a shot, unless you are particularly adept at the drop-shot, and that is the deep forcing drive or the hard, sharply angled crosscourt drive, which you follow to the net.

Never be tentative in returning a midcourt shot, and never retreat to the backcourt after making your return, for that is the essence of bad position play. Go for a winner, and in practicing, don't compromise if you are weak on these short shots. Learn how to put the ball away from this position. It involves only a slight raising of the racket head above the wrist on the backswing if the ball is high; and just the ordinary backswing if the ball is below shoulder height. Some players find it difficult to put the midcourt ball away, because they refuse to complete their stroke with the follow-through. Feeling crowded by their proximity to the net, they want to lift the low shots over with their wrists and flick the high ones down with their wrists. But the wrist action should be just the same from this position as it is in the backcourt.

Good position play is just as important to the defensive as the aggressive player. I think I may say that one of the major factors in my ability to win matches was my reliable retrieving from difficult positions, the result of anticipation. I knew where I ought to be and did not waste much time getting there. I knew, too, where to return the ball to make things as difficult as possible for my opponent. Nothing I ever did helped me more in planning for matches than to figure, on the diagram of a court, the possible replies to all possible shots. I do not pretend that I went on the court with the diagram, in detail, in my mind, but it did make me aware of the most effective returns.

The overuse of the short shots is a mistake many would-be tacticians make. A short shot is seldom of much use unless it is sharply angled and fairly hard-hit. In doubles, which I shall discuss in another part of this book, the soft, short angled shot has its place, but in singles, there is too much court for one player to defend to give value to this shot unless the opponent is hovering on the baseline. It is a shot well used after a long hard drive, or when the opponent is particularly weak on short shots. But the average good player can anticipate the shot when it is made too often and his reply is generally withering.

Let us study this question of short shots by means of Figures 22 and 23. First of all, in Figure 22, you have hit the ball to A. As soon as you have completed your stroke, you move to O which is your central position behind the baseline. The point marked D, as you can see, bisects the angle of widest returns—those from A to C and A to B. Now you do not want to move to D as soon as you hit the ball from the backcourt because, observing your intention, your opponent might drop-shot to E. But just before he hits the ball, when it is perhaps too late for him to alter his return, you move to D, where you are nearly within equal reach of C and B. If you had remained at O, you can see how much farther you would have been from C, a difficult shot, than from B. You can also see that if, after hitting

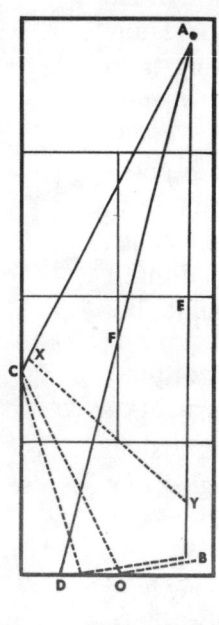

A. point at which ball is hit

A-B. opponent's return

A-C. opponent's alternate return

position play

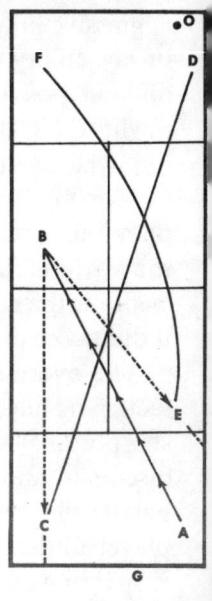

22.   23.

the ball to A, you had gone to the net; the point marked F, to the right of D, would have bisected the angle. It is important to realize that there is this difference in position for the backcourt and the net when covering the same shot.

In Figure 23, the opponent is at O and you hit a short shot crosscourt from A to B, immediately taking up a position at G. If your shot has bounced low, the opponent's return down the line from B-C will be risky, since the net is higher at the sides

60

than in the middle. He will most likely make a successful return to E. But if he does make the return B-C, your best reply is to take the ball on the rise, to quicken your reply, and drive it crosscourt to D. If, on the other hand, your opponent, having made the return B-C, rushes toward the middle of the net in fear of the crosscourt reply, your best return is back down the line. Nothing is more difficult on the court than to return quickly to a position you have just left. Weight, balance and momentum suddenly have to be switched, and in such a case the return down the line is too quick and direct to be covered successfully.

Now, if your opponent returns the ball from B to E, I know of no more effective reply than the lob from E to F, particularly if the lob has a low trajectory, just missing his racket, and carries pitch. The alternative replies depend on whether he moves slowly or rapidly to the middle of the net. If the former, the drive from E down the line is difficult to cover; if the latter, the crosscourt return back to B.

Important to good position play is an understanding of spin and its uses. Look at Figure 24 on page 62.

Top-spin—Any ball which spins forward has top-spin. In illustration A, the racket R is moving as the arrow indicates, across the back upper surface of the ball. As this movement of the racket causes the ball to spin forward *with* the direction of flight, the ball's tendency will be, after a certain distance, to drop rapidly forward. The more accentuated the spin, the sooner the ball will drop. There are two things that must be taken into consideration with regard to top-spin: they are *speed* and *degree* of spin, for they govern the kind of return you make.

If you are hitting from the backcourt and you strike the ball with great force, the racket moving as the arrow indicates, the ball will carry deep and, in all probability, not drop until it reaches the baseline or an approximate position. But if you hit with equal force, the racket coming up from below the ball's center and moving a greater distance across its back surface, the accentuation of the spin will decrease the ball's speed and there-

24.   spin of the ball

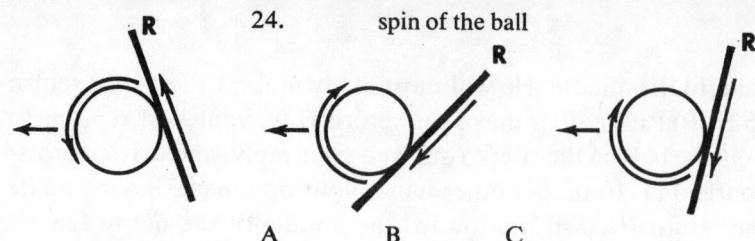

R is racket face, moving in direction indicated by arrow.

        D   E

R is racket face, moving forward from lower, back surface of ball.

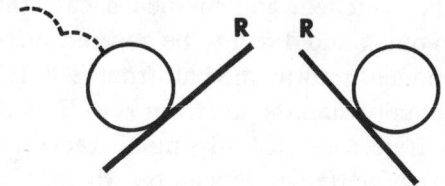

- A. Movement of closed racket face in hitting a sliced drive.
- B. Movement of open racket face in hitting a top-spin drive.
- C. Movement of slightly open racket face in making a chop stroke.
- D. Will bounce to the left.
- E. Will bounce to the right.

fore its air resistance, and the ball will, most likely, drop nearer the service line than the baseline.

If your intention, in using top-spin, is to drive your opponent well out of court beyond the baseline, you naturally make the speed of your shot greater than the spin. If you don't, this is what will happen: your shot will be too shallow, and its heavy spin will avail you little, for your opponent will take the ball as it rises from the ground—an easy shot to make off a top-spin drive—return it to the corner and go to the net. He will never, if he is smart, allow the ball to reach the maximum height of its bounce. If the ball carries only moderate top-spin and great speed, however, its depth will be assured. And if he waits on the bounce, the ball will have sufficient pitch to force him out of court, so even if he takes it on the rise, he will be making the return at a greater distance from you, giving you time to cover his shot, however fast.

The picture is quite different if your opponent is coming to the net against you. You want to make him volley up so that you can, in turn, drive down at him. The top-spin shot of moderate spin is very easy to volley, particularly when it is above the level of the net. So you want to exaggerate the spin and decrease the speed to catch him at his feet as he comes in. In this case, the closer your opponent gets to the net, the quicker you want your return to drop.

Now, let us assume that you are the receiver of the spin shot. You must learn to anticipate top-spin, and you can, if you watch the opponent's racket carefully. It is very difficult to disguise top-spin because the racket must begin below the level of the ball and move sharply up over it. The more sharply, the heavier the top-spin. The follow-through ending above the shoulder is also an indication of top-spin. *Invariably, the best way to handle the top-spin drive is to take the ball on the rise.* At the top of its bounce, the spin is almost nil and you have to make your own speed and pace, unassisted by any force of your opponent's shot, in addition to being forced to hit a high ball.

The constant use of top-spin should be avoided. But no ball crosses the net without spinning, however slightly; even the flat drive carries a little. This shot, by carrying the very minimum spin—either over- or underspin— travels the fastest through the air and is the strongest attacking weapon.

The most useful application of top-spin is in (1) slowing up the game when the opponent does not like to hit this type of shot; (2) gaining time for yourself by hitting deep and not too hard but with exaggerated spin; (3) eluding the incoming player by dropping the ball at his feet; (4) making a safe return when the margin for error is small.

Slice—In Figure 24-B the racket (R) is moving as the arrow indicates, from slightly above the level of the ball, down across its back, under surface. As this movement of the racket causes the ball to spin backward *against* the direction of its flight, it will travel through the air with less speed than the drive, its air resistance being less than the drive's. In addition to spinning backward, the sliced ball spins to one side on an imaginary axis parallel with the racket at the moment of impact; if you slice the ball on its right, under side, the imaginary axis will be parallel with the line R in D; if you slice it on its left, under side, the imaginary axis will be parallel with R in E. If you slice straight behind and under the ball, its imaginary axis will be approximately parallel with the net.

The bounce depends upon which side you slice the ball. If you slice it on the left side, it will bounce to the right; on the right side, it will bounce to the left; from directly behind, it will bounce forward. This knowledge of the bounce of the slice is important in attacking a weakness on either backhand or forehand, as you can see! As I said in the part of this book pertaining to the trimmings of the game, the slice must not be the foundation of your game. Because it travels through the air comparatively slowly, and tends to rise, due to its spin, as it crosses the net, it is an easy shot to volley, and except in unusual circumstances, is useless as a passing shot. Whereas it is possible to hit the flat drive through the narrowest of openings, it is difficult to play the slice with quite such accuracy, due to its spin and its susceptibility to wind.

The slice has very definite uses which should be borne in mind. They are (1) to slow down the game, since a slice cannot be taken on the rise and the opponent is forced to wait until the spin is considerably decreased; (2) to worry an opponent who cannot make effective returns of a sliced ball, or who prefers a waist-high ball to a very low one; (3) to clear the way to the net when the opponent makes good angled returns off straight drives; (4) to draw the opponent out of court for the next drive; (5) to take advantage of a wet, grass court, where the sliced shot skids more than on any other surface.

When you are learning how to slice, you must intersperse that practice with flat driving so that you are certain not to impair your timing or your confidence in the drive. Remember that the slice loses half of its effectiveness if it is not used in conjunction with the drive.

If you are the receiver of the slice, there are two things you must know: (1) never slice a slice; (2) never half-volley a slice. If you are playing an opponent who slices, go to the net as constantly as possible against him.

It is not difficult to anticipate an outright slice because of the motion of racket and arm in making the shot. Having anticipated it, do not make the mistake of running into the ball. Its low, skidding bounce is often deceptive and players are apt to move too close to the point at which they judge the ball will land. It is easier to compensate for an error in judging the bounce of the straight drive, which is high enough to allow time for compensation, than to rectify an error in judging the slice, which hangs low to the court and does not offer much time for adjusting your position or timing.

The sliced drive is harder to anticipate because it generally begins by resembling the flat drive, the upper edge of the racket head tilting back just as the ball is hit, or sometimes slightly before. That is why I stress watching the ball so closely. If you do, you will see it strike the inclined surface of your opponent's racket and be ready for the sliced drive.

Chop—In Figure 24-C you will notice that the racket R moves down the back surface of the ball and only very slightly under it. This motion of the racket increases somewhat the backspin of the ball, but tends to shorten its flight. It requires much more exertion to chop deep than to slice deep, which means that the chop is really more useful in making short crosscourt returns than in hitting to the baseline. In another way the chop differs from the slice. Its bounce is shorter, its tendency being to dig into the court rather than to skid. For this reason the chop stroke makes a better drop-shot than the slice stroke. The chop does not tend to rise as it crosses the net to the extent that the slice does; so if you are going to use one as a passing shot or a shot aimed at the feet of the incoming opponent, let it be the chop.

Here again, let me remind you that the chop is an auxiliary shot, useful for a change of pace, for making short crosscourt shots, for drawing the opponent out of position. But it should never replace the drive, nor should you use it when you can use the drive to better advantage.

Chapter IV

Proper Timing and a Method of Acquiring It

We have discussed in these pages those forces which can give power to your shots. They are, you will remember, the transfer of the body weight, the pivoting of the shoulders and the well-timed action of the hitting arm. There is another factor affecting the speed and pace of your shots and that is timing. It is important to understand this in relation to your game. If most of your shots are hit flat, it is really imperative for best results to take an early ball. If you use the fairly exaggerated top-spin drives, it is perhaps to the advantage of your spin to take the ball a little later because the less forward spin there is on the ball when you hit it, the more top-spin you can put on it.

All players using exaggerated top-spin have the tendency to hit the ball either at the top of its bounce or as it is dropping. This is one reason why I do not advocate consistent use of such spin.

There is much to be said in favor of taking the ball on the rise, as it comes up from the court before it has reached the top of its bounce. In so timing you benefit by the pace of your opponent's shot, whereas by waiting until it has reached the top of its bounce or is dropping, most of the pace of the opponent's shot is lost, forcing you to make your own pace on the return. Another advantage of early timing is in hurrying your opponent.

I think the best method of acquiring individual timing is by practicing in the following manner: first, determine on the average shot to hit the ball before it reaches the height of its bounce and well before that on the high-bouncing shot; then begin hitting the ball as soon as possible after it has begun to rise from the ground. In every successive shot delay your timing a fraction of a second until you are hitting the ball midway between the court and the top of the bounce. Somewhere in these successive points you will find the one at which you hit most effectively and have most confidence. When you have judged where this point is, count to yourself like this—"bounce . . . hit"; saying "bounce" when the ball strikes your court and "hit" when you hit it. This will establish a rhythm in your mind which you will soon follow subconsciously, so that if the bounce of the ball is slow, you will hit it sooner to keep the rhythm and if the bounce is fast you will not spoil the rhythm by letting the ball crowd you into hitting it too soon.

Probably because the senses work together—for example if you hear a sound, say the beat of a horse's hoofs or the noise of a motor, your eyes will follow that sound—you will find yourself watching the ball more closely while you are conscious of its audible impact on ground and racket.

The more quickly you can effectively and accurately hit the ball, which depends upon your individual eyesight and reflexes, the faster and more punishing game you will be able to play. But if you find yourself sacrificing accuracy by taking a very early ball, slow down your timing very slightly to accommodate the speed of your eye and reflexes. However, make certain, by consistent practice, that it is not possible for you to time your hit more quickly before you slow down, and decide only after you are convinced that no mechanical defect in your stroking which can be corrected is preventing quick timing.

Chapter V

Doubles

Good doubles play means good partnership; and good partnership implies two players understanding each other's games, having a fair estimation of each other's weakness and strength whether mechanical or physical and a willingness to sublimate oneself as an individual player to the common good of the team and a co-ordination of movement and of play.

Occasionally you will find two players who, though not the best of friends, make a good team, but this is rare and exists only when both are superlatively good doubles players and can curb their feelings for the sake of winning. Generally, the best teams have been players who enjoy each other's respect and friendship.

Margaret du Pont and Louise Brough were such a team, and very successful they were, winning the American doubles cham-

25. On a difficult volley, Ken McGregor's partner, Frank Sedgman, stands parallel with him and ready for the opponent's return. WORLD TENNIS

pionship twelve times. On the rare occasions when one of the members of this team was off form, the other was constantly encouraging, making it possible to pull out matches that might otherwise have been lost.

The compatibility of temperaments and games results in victory for other reasons, as well; one of the chief being that each partner tries to give the other a chance to bring off his best shot, and each tries to avoid making a shot, however brilliantly executed, that will put the other in difficulty.

How often you will see one partner on a team drive the ball with all his might at the opponent when he knows that the reply will be a volley past the other partner at the net. He has been unable to resist the temptation to show off his drive because the more effective slower dipping drive or the well-placed lob are less spectacular.

To take another case, you will frequently see one partner enjoying the applause which his brilliant overhead smash brings forth when it is his less conspicuous partner who has forced the lob which he has smashed. By his own stupidity, he will be led into believing that he is the dominating force on the court—one result of which is unwise "poaching" (or in tennis parlance, "hogging the court").

One of the greatest doubles players, man or woman, who ever lived is Elizabeth Ryan. Her record of victories in every tennis-playing country and her ten world championships with a variety of partners will probably never be equaled. Bunny Ryan was not a hard hitter; she did not confuse the opposition with powerful drives through small openings. In fact she usually chopped on both forehand and backhand, but she understood the tremendous value of angles in doubles play. I have had the pleasure of being Bunny Ryan's partner on many occasions and I know of no better way to describe perfect doubles play than to recount the manner in which she conducted our game.

In the first place, she was as much a stickler for getting the first service in as I remember George Lott, in my opinion the best of the men, to have been. Her reason was obviously sound and was twofold. For by this you save yourself a certain amount of energy in your service game and keep your opponent farther back in court than you will on your second serve. She believed, quite rightly, as George Lott did, that it is better to reduce the speed of your first service and get it in than to try to ace the opponent and take the chance of serving a fault. The pressure on the receiver is psychologically less severe when he is receiving the second service. The farther back he stands to receive service, the farther he must hit the ball to return it; and therefore the server has more time to reach the net simultaneously with the return. At least the server is less likely to be caught by the ball at his feet as he comes in.

To compensate for the lack of great speed on her service, Bunny invariably placed it at the most awkward point for the receiver. If the receiver was weak on the forehand, he would find the ball shooting out wide to the right; if he disliked to hit the ball close to him, he would find it curving in toward his body. In the meantime, Bunny was well in toward the net to make her formidable volley or smash.

Playing with Bunny, I found myself given one opportunity after another to win points on comparatively easy shots, particularly when she was receiving service and I was at the net. She would hit a low, skidding shot crosscourt past the opponent at the net. The incoming server would be forced, if he reached the ball at all, to volley up onto my racket. Sometimes on receiving service Bunny would make a return of the same kind, low and skidding, deep to the server's backhand, which would force a weak lob that I could smash for a winner.

Naturally, Bunny directed our play, and it was fascinating to see her confuse the opponents by a succession of sharply angled straight and dipping shots, lobs just out of reach that pitched forward on bouncing, deep lobs that dropped into the corners, angled volleys and smashes. She was ever alert to the possibility of opening up the court, whether by drawing both opponents to the center by hitting between them, or by forcing both out of court in anticipation of her widely angled slices, volleys and smashes.

Of course there are times, and I am sure Bunny realized it, when a severe service is invaluable. Donald Budge's ability to pull out an ace at the crucial point in a doubles match was frequently the deciding factor in the victory of his team. But if he had attempted to serve his cannon ball throughout the match, the exertion and the number of faults which would probably have resulted would have counterbalanced the advantage.

Too frequently one sees a player with a severe first service and a mediocre second serve. The first service, being hit with great force for the sole purpose of serving an ace, succeeds about one time in ten if it isn't accurate. On the majority of points, therefore, the easy service puts the ball in play; but the server thinks he has a good serve because now and then he manages to put the cannon ball in court. Such a serve is only useful when it is controlled.

The game of doubles, tactically speaking, really has little in common with the game of singles. The amount of court and the length of the net to be covered by each partner is so much less in doubles that the passing shots and volleys which earn points in singles cannot be expected to win them in doubles. One of the most common winning placements in doubles, particularly against players whose teamwork is uncertain, is the drive down the middle of the court. Unless a team has decided beforehand who is to handle this shot, the players both lunge for the ball, either missing it or making an ineffective return; or else, in confusion, letting the ball go by without an attempt to hit it.

In singles, the straight drive down the line is often an outright winner and always a difficult shot to reply to. In doubles it has value only when the partners are inclined to gravitate toward the center of the court. In singles, the server so rarely follows his service to the net, unless his delivery has made this advance advantageous, that the majority of returns are played deep, either crosscourt or down the line. In doubles, however, as the server nearly always follows his delivery to the net, the return must, for best effect, be played short crosscourt with the intention of catching the server at his feet as he comes up.

The constant purpose of the receiver should be to so place his return that he forces the server to volley up; and, naturally the receiver also tries to place the ball away from the server's partner who is at the net.

Except on the delivery of service, it is an unwritten rule in doubles that the partners must play parallel. If one is forced to run back in pursuit of a lob, the other should move back too, unless it appears that the lob may be returned offensively before it has bounced. At the first opportunity to return to the net, they should go up together. The reason for this is that there should be no gap in their court through which the ball can be sent. (See Figure 26.)

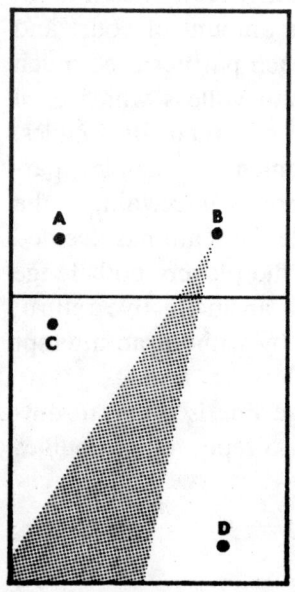

26.   parallel play

A-B.   partners holding net position

C.   opposing partner playing from net

D.   opposing partner playing back

Shaded area shows gap between *C* and *D,* through which ball may be hit by *B.*

Another doubles rule is this: seize the net position at the first opportunity and hold it. Try to dislodge the opponents from that position. If it is necessary to lob over the opponents' heads to get to the net, lob. The reason so many servers prefer the high-bouncing twist service to the flat one is that the former gives them more time to get in close to the net before the return can possibly pass them.

The straight powerful volley that is so often a winner in singles, does not present any problem to a good doubles team; but the angled volley is one of the best means of opening the opponents' court for the winning shot. The same is true of the smash. In singles the sheer speed of a straight smash is often enough to win a point, but in doubles, with two players covering the backcourt, it is apt to be returned by deep, well-placed lobs until the smasher misses the point. The angled smash is another story. Even if it is returned, the receiver has been driven far enough out of court to leave an opening for the next smash.

Anticipation is even more important in doubles than in singles because the play is so much faster. For example, if your partner is serving and the opponents are consistently hitting crosscourt, rather than lobbing to you or trying to pass you down your alley, you are tempted to poach. If you start to cross too quickly, you give the receiver time to change his direction and put the ball down your unguarded alley. You must closely watch the ball onto his racket, begin to cross over when it is too late for him to change direction, and having crossed, remain there.

It is up to your partner to defend the half of the court you have left by poaching, but if you then return to your original side, you force your partner to run back and forth across the baseline like a scared rabbit. You should never make a habit of poaching indiscriminately just for the fun of seeing how many winners you can make. Unless you put the ball away when you poach, you are in a far more vulnerable position than if you had left the ball to your partner. If you should make a weak return, a quick return by the opponent sharp across the court can only be reached by your partner by a miracle.

On the other hand, if you are playing against the net player who poaches, drive every now and then for his alley, even if he returns the drive for a winner, just to remind him that you are aware of his poaching. He will poach with less confidence, and in order to protect his alley, will not be so inclined to move toward the center of the court. Another good answer to the poacher is the lob. It will catch him badly off balance and force his partner, who has probably already run in toward the net, to retreat for the lob.

In doubles, always try to confuse the opponents, and concentrate on anticipating their usual returns of certain shots. If one or both opponents, when receiving service, invariably play the ball sharp across court, perhaps the best answer is the Australian formation: that which places the partner of the server in the same half of the court as the server and facing the partner of the receiver. (See Figure 27.) This formation blocks the opening for the crosscourt return, and forces the receiver to play his return down the line or to lob. You have, then, only two instead of three returns to anticipate.

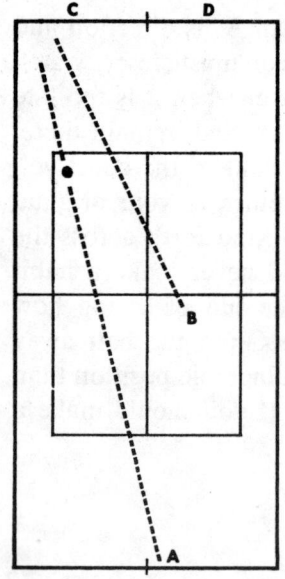

27.   Australian formation

A.   server

B.

Partner of server standing in same half of court, in position to cover crosscourt return by receiver C.

In choosing a partner, find one whose game complements your own. If you are weaker on one stroke than another, find a partner who is strong on your weakness. If you know that you lack great power, try to find it in your partner. And above all, choose one with whom you are temperamentally compatible. Practice together to make your games dovetail; try to foresee every contingency that might arise in a doubles match and plan accordingly how you can meet it and still preserve your teamwork, your effectiveness as a unit. When you are playing doubles, you are no longer playing an individual game. You are playing both for yourself and your partner; a harmonious and generous attitude is just as important as combining your knowledge of tactics.

Chapter VI

Strategy

One of the most important factors in tennis is strategy which differs from tactics. Tactics concern the purely mechanical defense of your court and the offensive against your opponent. Strategy deals with temperament, your own and your opponent's. It requires that you admit to yourself your weaknesses and your strength and that you are able to recognize these qualities and defects in your opponent as well. Strategy is a plan of campaign which takes into account your opponent's stamina, courage, nervousness and ingenuity. It is a preconceived plan for thwarting your opponent's best weapons as well as making it possible to get full value from your own.

There are players who cannot stand a series of long rallies. They are capable of playing three hard-fought sets so long as the rallies are only of moderate length. Once you wind them by a tremendously long exchange of shots, they lose all the effectiveness of their strokes for several points, and oftentimes that advantage to you may mean the match.

I have always felt that the longer a rally went on, the more important it was to win it from the psychological point of view. This is my reason: given equal strength and stamina, both players are going to be equally tired by such a rally, but the player who loses it is going to be disappointed, depressed or discouraged in addition. The more important the point, the more it is likely to affect his effort in the following point. Losing such a rally also discourages the opponent from resorting to further tests of steadiness.

I often used the slice for purposes of strategy rather than tactics. I knew that I was right because of the subsequent admission of many of my opponents—"I hate that shot." Whenever I met an opponent who had a rhythmic driving game and who, I knew, habitually practiced against drives, I usually hit a few slices to her to see how she reacted to the shot. If I found that it troubled or annoyed her, I made a mental note to save it for the crucial stages of the match.

One match particularly stands out in my mind. It is the semifinal round Dorothy Round and I played in the 1933 American championships. Both of us were eager to play Helen Wills Moody in the final. Dorothy had been playing exceptionally well during the tournament, so I wasn't sure about the outcome of our match. But I remembered from previous matches against her that she disliked playing against a slice. She had a long, low and very fast drive on both forehand and backhand. I liked to hit such shots, but as I had not been very well during the summer, I knew that my endurance would fail before hers did. So I decided that I would drive against her up to a point and then begin to slice, first to her forehand and then to her backhand. When I sliced to her backhand, I would go to the net. This plan worked well enough for me to win in three sets.

Very often a player who is sure of his overhead smash will err on it at the crucial point of a match. Two examples have convinced me of this fact. The first was in play against Sarah Palfrey (then Mrs. Cooke) in the final round of the American championship in 1935. I had won the first set and we were playing closely in the second. Knowing how much of Sarah's best game depended upon confidence, I didn't want the match to go to three sets. I was trying everything I could think of in the way of drives and slices and chops with little success. Finally I decided to try the lob. I continually brought her up to the net with short shots and lobbed to her backhand. She hit one after the other out of court. At first, she was so certain of her smash that she took insufficient care in making it. Her first errors seemed to break her confidence and thereafter she missed the shots apparently through a lack of confidence. On that, alone, I feel I won the match.

The second example was in play against Alice Marble in the Wimbledon semifinal of 1938, which I mentioned earlier. At four-all and game point for me in both sets the same thing happened. She forced me wide of the forehand corner from where I saw no possible return save a lob. Knowing the strength of her overhead, I felt that the point was already lost, but to my surprise, she took the ball too quickly and hit it out. When the same thing happened in the second set, I felt more confidence in the lob. She may have recognized the similarity of the situation. I do not know. In any case, she again hit a lob out, this time into the backstop, and that point gave me the second set and the match.

The player who thrives on a lead must, if possible in any way, be kept from achieving that lead. It is better to get ahead by steady driving, slicing, by going to the net or lobbing until you have gained the lead; then you can afford to take a few chances, knowing that your opponent is fighting discouragement as well as your game.

If you know that your opponent is not discouraged by your early lead, then you will do well to experiment with different shots and various placements to ferret out his preference for shots and his weaknesses, if any, of position play. If he dislikes to play the ball close to his body, you have the center theory to exploit. If he dislikes to hit on the run, you have the side-to-side placement. But if perhaps, instead of being bothered by that, he dislikes running up and back, you have the drop-shot and lob combination, and the short, angled and long, deep shot combination.

You must never go on court with a plan of campaign which you will rigidly enforce upon yourself regardless of circumstances. Your opponent may surprise you by having a good day on a backhand which has previously been weak; he may have anticipated your plan and prepared himself for it. You must train yourself to a versatility that will permit you to alter your plan without adversely affecting your confidence. You must, in your training, play against every type of game so that none will confuse you. You must understand every stroke that it is possible to make and know the answer to it, for only then will you be the complete player.

One thing you must always remember: bad court conditions and bad weather are theoretically equally bad for both opponents. It may be that the court is soggy when you had hoped to win on speed and pace. Although you are forced to alter your plan of attack to suit these heavy conditions, your opponent has had to do the same thing. Your strokes may be harder to control in the wind than your opponent's; but you can always decide to play the match chiefly from the net where the wind has less effect upon your shots. There is always a way to meet unpleasant conditions. On a heavy court you can slice or chop to tremendous advantage. The important thing is never to allow your opponent to feel that you are upset by such conditions. And never let him feel that decisions or other breaks of the game affect you, except to make you fight all the harder. If he knows that he is battling an imperturbable opponent, you have already won half the contest.

Chapter VII

Ten Lessons for Juniors

Since I have written in detail of strokes, the basic ones as well as the trimmings, the grips for those strokes and the way they should be hit, I would like to bring out in the following pages the most important things a young player must learn after he knows how to hit the tennis ball.

1. Don't Avoid Your Weak Strokes—Develop Them By Using Them.

Pretend that your backhand is weaker than your forehand, and use it as the object of this lesson. Never run around it to take the ball on the forehand. If you do, you will not be giving yourself a chance to improve your backhand. In addition, you will find yourself so far over in your left court that your right court will be open for a winning shot by your opponent, or you will be so off balance that your attempt to get to the return on your forehand side will not be effective.

28. An easy way to find the forehand grip (right to left)—consider the racket face as an extension of the palm of hand. Draw the hand down from the strings to the handle.

If you seem to be afraid of your backhand, your opponent will take advantage of your fear of this stroke.

29.   Position when waiting for service. Note bent knees and heels slightly off ground.

The only way you can improve and finally perfect a weak stroke is by using it at every opportunity in a game as well as by working on it with all your concentration in practice.

Don't say to yourself, "It's a weak stroke, so I'll steer the play away from it," because you can't always do that. Most players have one stroke that is stronger than the others—forehand stronger than backhand; smash stronger than service. Pick out the points in the stronger strokes that make them more effective and apply them to the weaker strokes.

These points, on the ground strokes, might be just confidence and the aggressive body position that confidence brings. Or it might be timing—the sureness in taking the ball as it bounces up from the court rather than waiting until it has reached the top of the bounce or is falling from that point. Whenever you wait too long to hit the ball, you can be sure that you don't have enough confidence in that stroke. So practice it from every position in court and against every type of shot it is possible for a practice partner to use against you.

30. The backhand should be as strong as the forehand. Be sure the body weight goes into the shot.

On the overhead strokes, you might hit a smash with greater power than your service because you do not have as much time to think about it and therefore your stroke is more relaxed and hit with greater ease. Also, because your opponent has tossed up the ball you are going to smash, you instinctively watch it more closely than the ball you yourself throw up to hit. Of course this proves how important it is to keep your eye on the ball from the moment it is in play until a point is over. But on some shots, the inexperienced player tends to watch the ball more closely than on others.

You will always know what your weak strokes are by the way in which you approach them. A hesitating approach means lack of confidence. The minute you feel that hesitation, start working to get rid of it.

2. Remember the Difference in Reach on Backhand and Forehand Strokes—Drive and Volley.

Since the reach is greater on the backhand than on the forehand strokes because the playing arm does not come across the body, it is important not to crowd the ball on the backhand side, whether on the groundstroke, the volley, the drive-volley or the smash.

If you remember this, you will save yourself a lot of steps getting to the ball, and will have less fear of the wide return to the backhand side of your court that you think is going to pass you.

Go back to the demonstration of why you have greater reach on backhand than forehand. Have someone hold a ball against the center of your racket strings at the forehand hitting position. Then, without moving toward the ball, shift your feet to the backhand position and bring your racket in to hit the ball. You will find that there is almost an arm's-length difference between the points of hitting on the two sides. Where on the forehand the racket met the ball in the person's hand, it will meet his shoulder on the backhand.

This difference in length of stroke, and therefore in retrieving, can make a great difference in winning or losing a point.

The next time you watch a tennis match, notice the difference in length between the players' reach on any shot taken on the backhand side and that taken on the forehand side.

This is one of several reasons why you ought to have confidence in the backhand strokes. The others have already been explained — the greater hitting power of the shoulder as the arm goes through the stroke without interference from the body; the simplicity of the footwork that naturally takes the right foot in first.

31. The reach is not as long on the forehand as on the backhand. Make up for this by taking the shoulder through with the shot.

I repeat, here, that if you can develop your backhand strokes to a point where they are equal to or better than your forehand strokes, you will always have the opponent at a loss, because attack is usually figured against the backhand side since most players' forehand strokes are better than those taken on the backhand side. Even if the two sides are only equal, your opponent would not have any clear point at which to strike for a winner.

3. Swing Your Body Weight into Every Stroke.

When you watch a great player in a match, you will notice how his body seems to swing forward into every stroke. The only time it doesn't is when he has been pushed back to make a stroke, or has to make the stroke out of position while on the run.

One of the reasons for this forward movement of body weight is that the backswing has been made early enough to give the player time to come into the ball as he hits.

There is another thing involved. The expert player, knowing how important it is to watch the ball the entire time it is in flight, sees it quickly enough to come forward as he hits it.

Here, again, is confidence. I remember many matches I played when the ball was so clear to me before I hit it that I wondered how I could have ever missed it. On those days my eye was "in," and the mistakes I made were not due to lack of sighting the ball, but to hitting a little too closely for the lines or bringing my shot too close to the net tape for the margin of error.

32. Body weight going with the stroke has made this a powerful smash.

On every shot in the game, the movement of the body into the stroke can be the one thing that gives a shot its greatest force. But this movement of weight has to go with the swing of the stroke. For example, if you bring your weight in before your arm has come forward toward the hitting point on the forehand, backhand or service, you have wasted your body movement.

There is a connection between thinking forward with your weight and thinking forward with your mind. A player who is not sure of himself will seldom move forward as if he means to attack. He will, more likely, hang back, trying to make sure of his shots, afraid to hit out and afraid of his opponent's returns. If you meet a player like this, you can win your match if you move forward with confidence on every stroke you make, even if the stroke you make is not the best one in your game.

4. Learn How To Conserve Your Energy.

"Going for everything" is not a wise thing to do in tennis. There are many times when the opponent's shot is so well-placed and so far away from you that chasing it only takes from you some of the strength you need for the closer points.

You must learn when to fight on till the "last ditch," and when to concede the hopeless point. But be sure not to consider a shot hopeless if there is a chance of getting to it. You are the best judge of your speed of foot and length of reach.

Certain points in a game are more important than others: for example, if you get to 15-0 it doesn't matter too much if you lose the next point. But if you get to 30-15, it matters very much, for if you win the point, you will then be at 40-15 which gives you two chances to make game. In other words, if you lose a point at 40-15, you will then be at 40-30 — only one chance for game and your opponent threatening to make deuce. These illustrate the points at which you should go all out to win, on the plus side.

Now take the minus side. If you are 0-15 down, you ought

to really extend yourself to get to fifteen all, for if you don't, your opponent's lead of 30-0, whether on your service or his, is a great mental advantage for him. At 0-30 against you he will think, "One more point and I will have forty-love—three chances for game by winning a single point." He is going to play much harder to make game or keep his lead than he will if he doesn't see game ahead of him—particularly at the important stages of a match.

33. Conserve your energy on the serve by stepping in as you hit. If your serve is good enough, go to the net. If it isn't, move back about a foot behind the baseline.

There are times when you walk from one service court to the other during which you can conserve your energy. Don't rush, because you want to get on with the next point; and don't walk too slowly to get your breath—that is not fair to your opponent. Walk at a normal pace, breathing deeply as you walk, and remember that you owe your opponent the courtesy of being ready to receive service when you arrive at the receiver's position and are facing him with your racket in position; or, if you are the server, you owe him the courtesy of being prepared to serve when he is ready to receive.

Don't forget that physical fitness is a part of the game. You should neither jeopardize your opponent nor allow yourself to be jeopardized by him because of any lapse of physical endurance. Among the many duties of the umpire is that of keeping play continuous with the exception of the pauses and intermissions allowed by the rules. The umpire is right when he orders a player onto the court if he has taken too long refreshing himself at the stand on the change-over between odd games, or directs play to begin when either or both players are stalling for time. The referee will see that the player taking too long in the dressing room between set intermissions is immediately escorted to the court, in the case of an important match, or told to be there at once or default, in the case of a lesser match. Thus, in a way, stupidly temperamental players are prevented from holding up play and jamming the schedule. And the spectators, who support the game, are given the right to see matches played as they should be.

These rules, enforced by umpire and referee, also equalize the chances of both players and make certain that, as far as they have control, the best player wins.

It is true that the player who conducts his game along the lines of real sportsmanship, which is, after all, only reasonable consideration of the other fellow, conserves his energy in many ways.

5. A Double-Fault Is a Tennis Crime.

As I mentioned earlier, a double-fault has been called a tennis crime, and with good reason, for it is a point just given to your opponent. Had the second ball been put into play, even though not very effectively, the opponent might have made an error or you might at least have had a chance of winning the following exchange.

It is for this reason that you must develop a reliable second service. It should carry some spin—either top-spin or the back-spin of a slice. If your opponent is weaker on the backhand than the forehand, concentrate on the top-spin second service;

if he is weaker on the forehand, concentrate on the slice. But alternate them sufficiently to keep him guessing and to prevent his getting used to one or the other.

Your "big gun," of course, should be the powerful first service, hit flat; but if you find that your opponent is beginning to adjust his timing to handling it, vary it with a spin service. This is good tactics for two reasons: it will force him suddenly to change his timing; and if he has been standing fairly far back of the baseline to take your flat service, he is apt to be put off good balance as he is forced into the right for the slice, or wide to the left for the top-spin.

Don't forget that many factors enter into the delivery of a successful service. You are in the "driver's seat" when you put the ball into play if you make its placement mean something in your over-all plan for the point. As a rule, your opponent starts the point on the defensive, and you have the chance of capitalizing on his stroke weaknesses. If he does not seem to have any, at least you have the chance to open up his court for a winning placement. An opponent's failure to return service often breaks his concentration and confidence and you are then halfway to victory.

Whether your service is the flat, powerful one or the spin service, be sure that it is made as effortlessly as possible. This will come from proper footwork, timing, balance and the use of your body weight as you come into the hit.

6. The Volley Must Be an Offensive Shot.

The volley will probably be a losing shot if it is made defensively. So there is no use in going to the net if you have only a fifty-fifty chance, or less, of making it count. The purpose of the shot is twofold: either to make the winner with the first volley, or to prepare, by placement, to make it with the second. Otherwise, you will be forced back by the lob or passed by the line or crosscourt drive.

Don't forget that when you are in the volleying position, you are open to the crosscourt on either forehand or backhand side, so the approach shot behind which you go to the net, whether it is service or drive, must be well placed; and you must watch the ball especially carefully as your opponent hits it, in order to anticipate his return and get into position for it before it reaches the net, if possible.

Punch your volley with the minimum of backswing. Because the ball is taken before it strikes the ground, there is not time for preparation of the stroke as there is in the groundstrokes. And for the best effect, your racket must meet the ball when it is in front of you.

As a rule, the ball should be hit flat, particularly when passing an incoming opponent or when placing the ball to an opening in his backcourt. The sliced or undercut volley is useful if the skidding shot that results carries the ball out of reach of the opponent.

Never be hesitant about the volley. Think aggressively when you make it.

7. Timing Is the Secret of the Powerful Smash.

The only way to develop your sense of judgment of the depth and height of the lob and how you can best smash it is to practice against lobs. Have someone go out on the court with you and hit lobs to you at every possible positon, height and depth. Watch the ball very closely, and time your pace to get to it so that you are approximately in a serving position when you hit it.

There are times when the lob you are going to smash will be well over your head. You may have to leap for it, or run back to smash it after the bounce. Then, of course, your body movement cannot be the same as it is for the service. Your body motion as you hit the ball must be forward, however, if only from the waist up, to give it the necessary power.

Needless to say, placement is of the greatest importance in smashing; and timing—hitting the ball slightly in front of your head, with fully extended arm—makes desired placement less difficult.

Whether you take the ball with or without leaping for it, practice timing the stroke so that you are not hitting the ball behind your head or, on the other hand, too far out in front of you. And when you hit the ball, do not be hesitant. Try to kill it, to win outright with it, for that will discourage your opponent from subjecting you to a lobbing attack.

8. The Lob Has Many Uses.

The lob is the only shot that can be made as effectively when going back from the ball as when going toward it. The reason for this is that no body weight is required for the shot, for it is made simply with the arm, its effectiveness resulting from its position, its trajectory and its timing.

The trajectory need not always be high. Judgment of its height must be based on the opponent's position. If he is rushing to the net, sometimes the lob just out of reach and pitching a little after the bounce will be the winner; if he is already entrenched at the net, the high lob is the proper one to make.

The lob is not made only from the backcourt. Very often, it can be made with great effectiveness as an offensive weapon from midcourt if it has the element of surprise.

As for any slowing of the ball's pace, the opponent must alter his timing. The lob will break the rhythm of quick timing, which many opponents will find difficult to get back and will therefore be apt to mishit a ball bouncing off the ground after a succession of lobs.

Although the lob is made with an open-faced racket, it is possible to apply top-spin by coming up sharply over the back of the ball as the racket rises in the air. This top-spin will cause the ball to pitch high and forward rapidly after the bounce.

Remember that although the lob can be an offensive return, it is primarily a defensive one. When using it to gain time for recovery of breath, you give away to your opponent the fact that you are tired; when using it to regain position, it is a strategic shot.

9. Use the Slice to Break the Opponent's Timing.

The slice should not be used without a reason. Its chief purpose is to break the opponent's timing, to slow down a driving attack and to affect the opponent's rhythm.

As a rule, it should be a deep shot. But the short, crosscourt slice can be a winner when the opponent is hovering on the baseline. The value in going to the net behind a slice lies in the relatively slow speed of the ball, giving you a chance to get in before the ball has bounced. In addition, the skidding spin of the ball makes a hard-hit driving return very difficult, and it is not easy to place the ball with accuracy.

Since the slice tends to bounce away from the opponent, its placement to the corners of the backcourt will force him to reach for the ball, limiting the power of his return. A slice to the center of the baseline can be very awkward for the opponent when he is running back from either corner, for it is difficult to anticipate the bounce of a sliced ball and he is likely to overrun.

The danger of overusing the slice is that it may affect the timing of your own drive. Also, overuse may enable the opponent to become accustomed to the action of the bounce and to readjust his timing to it.

Never slice a slice. If you do, you reverse the spin of the ball and you will be lucky if it reaches the net. And never slice against an opponent who is at the net, for the ball travels too slowly to elude him.

10. Use the Chop for Short Angles.

The chop is most useful when played at an angle into the opponent's forecourt. Unlike the slice, the bounce of the ball is rather dead and heavy, and if the stroke is made with a very rapid downward motion, the ball frequently tends to bounce back toward the net.

The chop travels through the air slower than the slice. For this reason, particularly, it is less effective than the slice as a deep shot. Its spin is not as disturbing as the slice, and it is inclined to sit up too much.

By shifting the racket face, while hitting, from the back of the ball to its far outer surface, the crosscourt to the opponent's forehand is easily made. By hitting from the inside, the crosscourt placement to the opponent's backhand is accomplished.

These placements are very effective when the opponent is coming into net against you, for it is difficult to return the spinning ball with power and accuracy. Its quick drop over the net forces the opponent to volley, giving you a chance to volley past him in return.

In returning a chop, as with a slice, do not try to chop or slice the ball. Hit it as hard as possible, and give it a good margin of error over the net.

In making the chop, as in making the slice, do not forget that your body weight must go into the shot. Don't make either shot with the arm alone.

Chapter VIII

The Final Word

1. Watch the ball.
2. Hit the ball approximately a foot in front of you.
3. As you hit the ball, transfer your body weight from the back to the forward foot.
4. Keep the racket on a line with the ball.
5. Keep your wrist firm.
6. Pivot on your hips and turn your shoulder to the net as you prepare to hit the ball.
7. Always follow through after hitting the ball.
8. Never let the ball crowd you.
9. Avoid long strides on the court.
10. Never change a winning game; always change a losing game.

Suggested Racket Weights and Balances

Age	Weight of Racket	Balance of Racket	Handle
9-13	11-12½ ounces	13 inches from end of handle	when holding racket, thumb should touch 1st joint of 2nd finger
14-17	13-13½ ounces		
18 on	13½-14¾ ounces	13 inches from end of handle to even balance	

Glossary

Ace: a winning shot the opponent cannot touch

Backcourt: the court between base- and service lines

Backhand: a stroke made from the left side (by a right-handed player)

Chop: a backspinning shot made as if one were chopping wood

Doubles: the game played by partners, two on each side of the net, using the full court

Double-fault: both serves hit into the net and/or over the service lines

Drive-volley: a volley usually made between shoulder- and head-level with a longer backswing than the conventional volley

Drop-shot: a backspinning shot made with delicate wrist action that causes the ball to drop just over the net with very little bounce

Fault: an error on service when the ball either goes into the net or over the service lines

Foot-fault: an error made by the server according to official U.S.L.T.A. rules, such as stepping on or over the service line before the ball has been hit

Forecourt: the court between service line and net

Forehand: a stroke made from the right side (by a right-handed player)

Half-volley: a shot made immediately after the ball bounces

Let: a point replayed, such as a service that hits the net cord and bounces in the opponent's service court; or a point replayed by decision of the umpire because of interference or other allowable reasons

Lob: a shot that hits the ball over the opponent's head

Lob-volley: a volley made to hit the ball over the opponent's head

Midcourt: the court area between extreme backcourt and forecourt

Overhead: any ball hit over the head, except service

Pace: the swiftness with which the ball bounds off the court

Service: the overhead stroke made from the baseline that puts the ball into play

Slice: a backspinning shot made as if one were slicing ham on the diagonal

Smash: an overhead

Speed: the swiftness with which the ball travels through the air

Strategy: the "campaign plan" for playing a match, which takes into account all of the opponent's weaknesses—technical, physical and psychological

Tactics: the means of accomplishing strategy

Timing: the interval between the bounce of the ball and the impact

Volley: a shot made before the ball touches the court

Officials in Tournament Play

A. *Referee:* the official who conducts a tournament and makes the decisions on questions during match play

B. *Umpire:* the official who scores a match and makes decisions that are not the responsibility of the referee

C. *Net-cord judge:* the official who judges when the ball has hit the net cord on service

D. *Linesmen:* the officials who call balls out on base-, side- and service lines

Bibliography

CONNOLLY, MAUREEN. *Power Tennis.* New York: A. S. Barnes & Co., 1954.

DRIVER, HELEN. *Tennis for Teachers.* Philadelphia: W. B. Saunders Co., 1938.

——————. *Tennis Self-Instructor.* Madison, Wisc., 1953.

MACE, WYNN and TYLER MICOLEAU. *Tennis Techniques Illustrated.* New York: A. S. Barnes & Co., 1952.

MURPHY, BILL *and* CHET MURPHY. *Tennis for Beginners.* New York: Ronald Press Co., 1958.

POTTER, NED. *World's Leading Players.* New York: World Tennis Magazine, published annually.

TALBERT, BILLY and BRUCE OLD. *The Game of Doubles in Tennis.* New York: Holt, Rinehart & Winston, 1956.

BIOGRAPHIES:

GIBSON, ALTHEA. *I Always Wanted to be Somebody.* Edited by Ed Fitzgerald. New York: Harper & Brothers, 1958.

GONZALES, PANCHO, *Man with a Racket.* New York: A. S. Barnes & Co., 1959.

MULLOY, GARDNER. *The Will to Win.* New York: A. S. Barnes & Co., 1960.

TALBERT, BILLY. *Playing for Life.* Boston, Mass.: Little, Brown & Co., 1958-59.

Index

American twist, 34
arm action, 16, 17, 34, 50, 66

backhand drive, 9, 10, 24-30, 80-84
basic strokes, 9-49
body balance, 19, 20, 27, 28, 43
body weight, 34
Borotra, Jean, 49
Brough, Louise, 69
Budge, Donald, 10, 21, 29, 31, 32, 36, 38, 54, 71

center theory, 41, 56, 78
change of pace, 65
chop, 49, 50, 52, 65, 79, 91, 92
Cochet, Henri, 12, 49, 53
Continental backhand grip, 24
Continental forehand grip, 12, 14, 50

Danzig, Allison, 38
doubles, 68-75
drive-volley, 40
drop shot, 49, 52, 53, 58
drop volley, 40, 56
Du Pont, Margaret, 69

Eastern forehand grip, 12, 16
Eastern backhand grip, 24, 25

forehand drive, 9, 10, 12, 14, 15, 29, 35, 38, 59, 80-84
follow-through (backhand), 25, 28, 59
follow-through (chop), 52
follow-through (drop-shot), 53
follow-through (forehand), 20, 59
footwork, 17, 19, 27, 34
forcing play, 8
Fraser, Neale, 58

Gonzales, Pancho, 12, 58

half-volley, 49, 53
Holcroft Watson, Mrs., 40

Johnston, Bill, 49

keenness, 8
Kramer, Jack, 12
Lacoste, René, 12, 49
legwork, 19
Lenglen, Suzanne,
lob, 43, 46, 47, 70, 73, 74, 77, 89, 90
Lott, George, 47, 70

Marble, Alice, 31, 32, 38, 78
Midwestern backhand grip, 25
Midwestern forehand grip, 25
Moody, Helen Wills, 38, 77

pace, 29, 66
Palfrey, Sarah, 77
Perry, Fred, 12, 53
physical fitness, 86, 87
poaching, 73, 74
position play, 54-65

reach, 82-83
Richards, Vincent, 49
Riggs, Bobby, 46
Round, Dorothy, 77
Ryan, Elizabeth, 69, 70, 71

service, 9, 30, 32-36, 54, 56-63, 84, 87, 88
slice, 35, 49, 50, 52, 63-65, 77, 79, 91
smash, 25, 28, 43, 63-65, 82, 84, 89
spin, 54, 61-63, 65, 66
strategy, 76-80

Tilden, Bill, 9, 12, 21, 29, 31, 32, 49
timing, 66, 67, 81, 89
touch, 8
top-spin, 34, 35
toss (service), 34
trimmings, 49-54

Vines, Ellsworth, 12
volley, 36, 38-41, 73
Von Cramm, 36

Western backhand, 24, 47
Western forehand, 14, 15, 38, 47
Wills, Helen, 26, 38
wrist, 50

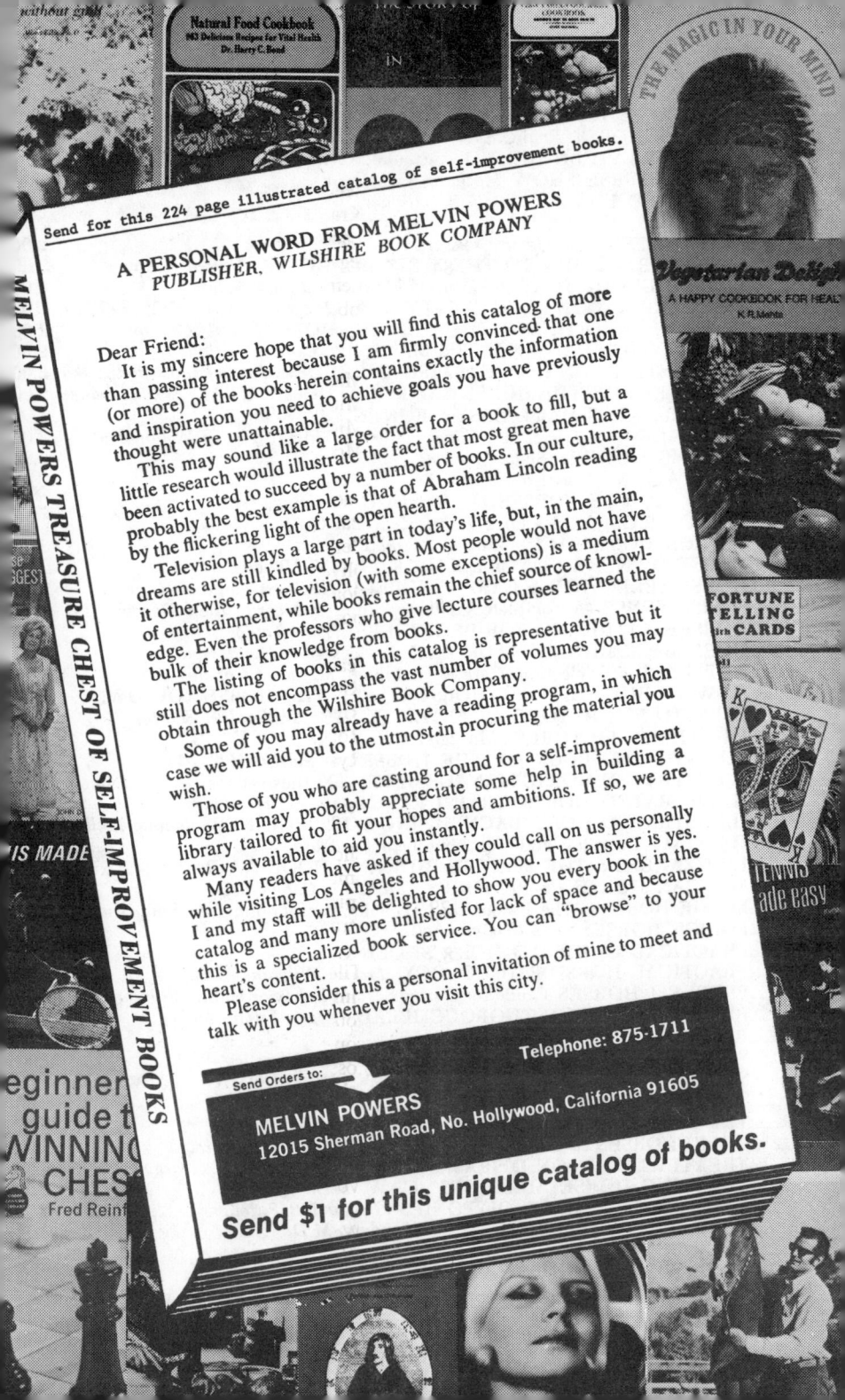

WILSHIRE HORSE LOVERS' LIBRARY

____	AMATEUR HORSE BREEDER A. C. Leighton Hardman	2.00
____	AMERICAN QUARTER HORSE IN PICTURES Margaret Cabell Self	2.00
____	APPALOOSA HORSE Bill & Dona Richardson	2.00
____	ARABIAN HORSE Reginald S. Summerhays	2.00
____	ART OF WESTERN RIDING Suzanne Norton Jones	2.00
____	AT THE HORSE SHOW Margaret Cabell Self	2.00
____	BACK-YARD FOAL Peggy Jett Pittinger	2.00
____	BACK-YARD HORSE Peggy Jett Pittinger	2.00
____	BASIC DRESSAGE Jean Froissard	2.00
____	BEGINNER'S GUIDE TO THE WESTERN HORSE Natlee Kenoyer	2.00
____	BITS—THEIR HISTORY, USE AND MISUSE Louis Taylor	2.00
____	BLOND GIRL WITH BLUE EYES LEADING PALOMINO (47"x27" poster)	5.00
____	BREAKING & TRAINING THE DRIVING HORSE Doris Ganton	2.00
____	CAVALRY MANUAL OF HORSEMANSHIP Gordon Wright	2.00
____	COMPLETE TRAINING OF HORSE AND RIDER Colonel Alois Podhajsky	3.00
____	DISORDERS OF THE HORSE & WHAT TO DO ABOUT IT Elsie Hanauer	2.00
____	DOG TRAINING MADE EASY & FUN John W. Kellogg	2.00
____	DRESSAGE—A study of the Finer Points in Riding Henry Wynmalen	3.00
____	DRIVING HORSES Sallie Walrond	2.00
____	EQUITATION Jean Froissard	3.00
____	FIRST AID FOR HORSES Dr. Charles H. Denning, Jr.	2.00
____	FUN OF RAISING A COLT Rubye & Frank Griffith	2.00
____	FUN ON HORSEBACK Margaret Cabell Self	3.00
____	HORSE OWNER'S CONCISE GUIDE Elsie V. Hanauer	2.00
____	HORSE SELECTION & CARE FOR BEGINNERS George H. Conn	2.00
____	HORSE SENSE—A complete guide to riding and care Alan Deacon	4.00
____	HORSEBACK RIDING FOR BEGINNERS Louis Taylor	3.00
____	HORSEBACK RIDING MADE EASY & FUN Sue Henderson Coen	2.00
____	HORSES—Their Selection, Care & Handling Margaret Cabell Self	2.00
____	HOW TO BUY A BETTER HORSE & SELL THE HORSE YOU OWN	2.00
____	HOW TO ENJOY YOUR QUARTER HORSE Williard H. Porter	2.00
____	HUNTER IN PICTURES Margaret Cabell Self	2.00
____	ILLUSTRATED BOOK OF THE HORSE S. Sidney (8½" x 11½")	10.00
____	ILLUSTRATED HORSE MANAGEMENT—400 Illustrations Dr. E. Mayhew	5.00
____	ILLUSTRATED HORSE TRAINING Captain M. H. Hayes	5.00
____	ILLUSTRATED HORSEBACK RIDING FOR BEGINNERS Jeanne Mellin	2.00
____	JUMPING—Learning and Teaching Jean Froissard	2.00
____	LIPIZZANERS & THE SPANISH RIDING SCHOOL W. Reuter (4¼" x 6")	2.50
____	MORGAN HORSE IN PICTURES Margaret Cabell Self	2.00
____	MOVIE HORSES—The Fascinating Techniques of Training Anthony Amaral	2.00
____	POLICE HORSES Judith Campbell	2.00
____	PRACTICAL GUIDE TO HORSESHOEING	2.00
____	PRACTICAL HORSE PSYCHOLOGY Moyra Williams	2.00
____	PROBLEM HORSES Guide for Curing Serious Behavior Habits Summerhays	2.00
____	RESCHOOLING THE THOROUGHBRED Peggy Jett Pittenger	2.00
____	RIDE WESTERN Louis Taylor	2.00
____	SCHOOLING YOUR YOUNG HORSE George Wheatley	2.00
____	STABLE MANAGEMENT FOR THE OWNER-GROOM George Wheatley	3.00
____	TEACHING YOUR HORSE TO JUMP W. J. Froud	2.00
____	THE LAW AND YOUR HORSE Edward H. Greene	3.00
____	TRAIL HORSES & TRAIL RIDING Anne & Perry Westbrook	2.00
____	TREATING COMMON DISEASES OF YOUR HORSE Dr. George H. Conn	2.00
____	TREATING HORSE AILMENTS G. W. Serth	2.00
____	WONDERFUL WORLD OF PONIES Peggy Jett Pittenger (8½" x 11½")	4.00
____	YOUR FIRST HORSE George C. Saunders, M.D.	2.00
____	YOUR PONY BOOK Hermann Wiederhold	2.00
____	YOUR WESTERN HORSE Nelson C. Nye	2.00

The books listed above can be obtained from your book dealer or directly from Melvin Powers. When ordering, please remit 25c per book postage & handling. Send one dollar for our 224 page illustrated catalog of self-improvement books.
Melvin Powers, 12015 Sherman Road, No. Hollywood, California 91605